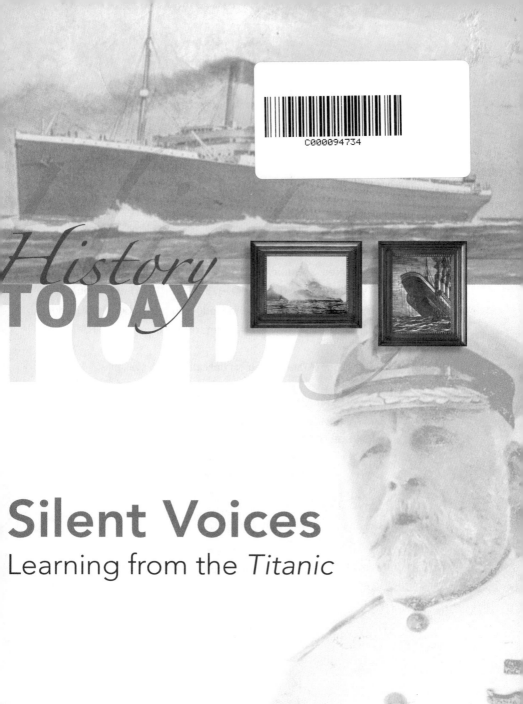

History
TODAY

Silent Voices

Learning from the *Titanic*

Clive Anderson & Ann Sloane

DayOne

© Day One Publications 2012
First printed 2012

ISBN 978–1–84625–315–7

British Library Cataloguing in Publication Data available

Published by Day One Publications
Ryelands Road, Leominster, HR6 8NZ
☎ 01568 613 740 FAX 01568 611 473
email—sales@dayone.co.uk
web site—www.dayone.co.uk
North America—email—usasales@dayone.co.uk

Cover design by Wayne McMaster
Printed by Orchard Press Cheltenham Ltd

'The sinking of the Titanic is one of those defining moments of human history which will always haunt and intrigue us. The great ship that was once the very symbol of man's self-confidence now lies at the bottom of the sea, a testimony to false hope, human arrogance and poor judgement. Ann and Clive have turned childhood fascination and careful research into a powerful and easily readable account of this momentous tragedy, giving us the facts we need to know alongside challenging spiritual application. They are not afraid to ask hard questions and to admit where mystery still persists. Above all, the spiritual lessons and powerful application of God's Word remind us of our fallibility, sinfulness and our absolute need to be right with our Maker through faith in His own Son, the Lord Jesus Christ.'

Ian Cooper, Pastor, Tollgate Evangelical Church, Surrey, UK

'Even as a child, I loved the sea, and, with it, have had an endless fascination for boats and ships. The Titanic was an amazing ship, a symbol of man's achievement in its day. So why the tragedy?

This book is a fresh look at one of the most emotive passenger ships ever built. Let the authors walk you through the story of the Titanic: the what ifs, the buts. Perhaps, in some way, you will see God in the acts of those who were there.'

Chris Duncan, Managing Director, Duncan Yachting Limited, Hampshire, UK

Dedication

Dedicated to John Mason
Father, friend, and inspiration for this book

Contents

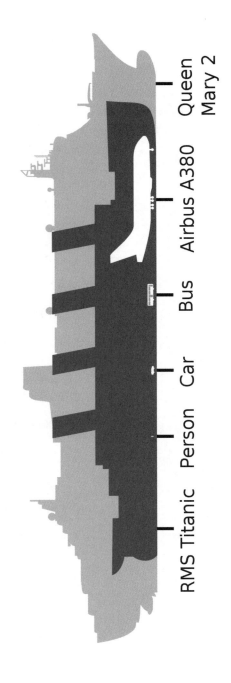

RMS Titanic   Person   Car   Bus   Airbus A380   Queen Mary 2

The size of RMS *Titanic* in comparison to familiar objects

The Great *Titanic*

It was on one Monday morning just about one o'clock,
When the great *Titanic* began to reel and rock;
People began to scream and cry,
Saying, 'Lord, am I going to die?'

> *Chorus*
> *It was sad when that great ship went down;*
> *It was sad when that great ship went down.*
> *Husbands and wives and little children lost their lives.*
> *It was sad when that great ship went down.*

It was sad when the ship left England; it was making for the shore.
The rich had declared that they would not ride with the poor.
So they put the poor below;
They were the first to go.

> *Chorus*

While they were building, they said what they would do;
We will build a ship that water can't go through.
But God, with power in hand,
Showed the world that it could not stand.

> *Chorus*

Those people on that ship were a long way from home.
With friends all around, they didn't know that the time had come.
Death came riding by;
Sixteen hundred had to drown.

> *Chorus*

The Great *Titanic* song

While Paul was sailing his men around,
God told him not a man should drown.
If you trust and obey,
I will save you all today.
> *Chorus*

You know it must have been awful with those people on the sea.
They say that they were singing *Nearer My God To Thee*.
While some were homeward bound,
Sixteen hundred had to drown.
> *Chorus*

American folk song (c. 1915)
Titanic Song as reported in *White's American Negro Songs* (1928)[1]

Note

1 Song about the great *Titanic* as reported in *N I White's American Negro Songs* (Harvard University Press, 1928)

Ships and shipwrecks

'God said to Noah, "... make yourself an ark of cypress wood,"' (Genesis 6:13–14).

RMS *Titanic* under construction in Harland & Wolff shipyards, Belfast

From the very first time that man set sail in a boat until the present day, there have been disasters at sea: shipwrecks, fires, torpedoes, collisions. Many people have lost their lives. There are many incredible stories which have been told about these disasters but the *Titanic* seems to be the one that fascinates the most. Why is that? Who can truly say? There have been other ships that have struck icebergs and have gone down with all hands. There have been disasters with far greater losses of life. But none resonate through time more than this one. The reason for this is probably the mass media—the ability to communicate news speedily across sea, as well as land, meant that many would hear about the disaster within a few hours of the *Titanic* sinking.

For those living in 1912, it was as great a shock as 9/11 was in 2001, when two aircraft hit the World Trade Center in New York, and the world watched the disaster unfolding on their television screens.

Personal interest

Ann's fascination with the *Titanic* began at the age of ten, when her father lent her one of his books to read; Walter Lord called it *A Night to Remember*. She says, 'I found the whole thing spellbinding: the story of a floating palace, a little world in itself, with people from every walk of life and from all over the world on board. It typified man's absolute confidence in himself and in his own achievements.' For Clive, it was remembering his grandfather (born 1888) speaking about it and how people used to think that they were invincible. His interest was further aroused upon seeing a picture of the *Titanic* superimposed across Trafalgar Square in London, and with that came the realization of just how large the ship had been.

The beginning

The *Titanic's* story probably began in the early 1900s. It was an age of great energy. Queen Victoria reigned over an empire comprising one quarter of all lands and peoples on earth. Its trade and industrial drive made Victorian Britain the world's richest nation. It was a country which was broadening its democracy and increasing its range of slow, but significant, social reforms. Queen Victoria's passing in 1901 brought an end to one era, but ushered in the beginning of another.

Edward VII came to the throne at the age of fifty-nine. He revived the monarchy's splendour, which had been in decline during Victoria's years of seclusion. He was politically aware and worked to reinforce Britain's position in Europe. He failed, however, to make friends with his nephew, Kaiser Wilhelm II of Germany. This aroused suspicions in Germany concerning Britain's long-term plans and was a factor which contributed to the start of the disastrous war in 1914.

However, before those tragic events unfurled, the Edwardians basked in a time of great self-confidence, which is exemplified in the song, *The Life I lead*, sung by David Tomlinson in the film *Mary Poppins*.

'It's grand to be an Englishman in 1910;
King Edward's on the throne.
It's the age of men;
I'm lord of my castle,
The sovereign, the liege!
I treat my subjects: servants, children, wife,
With a firm but gentle hand.
Noblesse Oblige!'[1]

An incredible world

Many wonderful new inventions and innovations were fostering the belief in the supremacy of man over nature. The Zeppelin, the escalator, air conditioning and lie detectors had all made an appearance. Thomas Edison was demonstrating his moving pictures and Louis Blériot had flown across the English Channel. Albert Einstein had published his theory of relativity ($E = mc^2$), and the Model T Ford was now being commonly sold.

In 1906 the British battleship HMS *Dreadnought* was launched, her armour, speed and guns rendering all other battleships obsolete; Britain truly 'ruled the waves'. However, with the inception of the Sopwith Aviation Company, a new form of travel was making headlines in 1912. From that time, ships would face increasing competition from air travel.

On 14 December 1911, Roald Amundsen had reached the South Pole. On 16 March 1912, Lawrence Oates—of the British Expedition to the same region, led by Robert Falcon Scott—left the tent uttering the immortal words: 'I am just going outside and may be some time.' By doing this, he gave his life in the hope that it would enable his friends to reach safety. Tragically, they did not survive either.

King George V ascended to the throne of England on 6 May 1910. He was nicknamed 'the Sailor King'. William Howard Taft, a distinguished jurist, effective administrator, but a poor politician, was President of the United States.

Not a perfect world

In 1902 a tragedy occurred at Ibrox Park in Glasgow. A large number of football supporters had been packed into the main stand for a Scotland versus England football match when the stand collapsed, killing twenty-six men and injuring over five hundred.

Across the world, war broke out between Russia and Japan on 6 February 1904. Although Russia was a much larger country than Japan, it did not have as many troops stationed in critical areas. This proved costly. Russia sent a fleet from the Baltic Sea around Africa and across the Indian Ocean where it was met by the Japanese at Tsushima Straits. There it was virtually annihilated. This was a precursor of troubles to come later in the century.

In 1906 a severe earthquake hit San Francisco in the USA. This was, perhaps, a reminder that man was not invincible. Sadly, the lesson was soon forgotten.

The early years of the twentieth century were a time of optimism in the western world. The novels of P. G. Wodehouse give the age a permanent glow, though regrettably, there was a darker side. A new scepticism concerning God seemed to be abroad—'Who needed him when man could achieve so much?'

Many thought of the *Titanic* and her sister ship, *Olympic*, as the epitome of human achievement. With such stupendous vessels crossing the Atlantic, nothing seemed beyond the scope of man's ingenuity. Tragically, a great and painful lesson had to be learnt by the people of that generation.

Does history repeat itself?

Is there any value in studying past events apart from their obvious element of interest or entertainment? Can the events that took place that night help us today in any way? We believe they can. Human nature being what it is, we are all prone to make the same mistakes our forefathers did; the essential human qualities do not change from one generation to another.

As it was with the events of 9/11, so it was for those who first heard the news of the loss of that great ship—large numbers were profoundly shocked. Abel, the first man to be murdered, has lain silent in his grave for a very long time, but the Bible states that 'by faith he still speaks, even though he is dead' (Hebrews 11:4). All involved in the *Titanic* are no longer able to speak, but the tragic events of April 1912 have much to teach each succeeding generation. Although there may be advances in many areas of life, we have the same emotions and desires as those who have gone before us. It is, therefore, unwise to ignore the past, considering it as being archaic and irrelevant. We should take careful note of the words of Sir Winston Churchill. He said, *'Those that fail to learn from history are doomed to repeat it.'*[2]

Chapter 1

Notes

1 Words of the song *The life I lead,* taken from the film *Mary Poppins,* produced by the Walt Disney Corporation, 1964 (composers: Richard M. Sherman and Robert B. Sherman)

2 Words of **Sir Winston Churchill** quoted from the Article 'The Great Depression and its downward economic Spiral': Part 1 of 3 by **Miriam B. Medina,** found at ezinearticles.com/?The-Great-Depression-And-Its-Downward-Economic-Spiral:-Part-1-Of-A-3-Part-Series&id=6430877

Men who go down to the sea in ships

'Others went out on the sea in ships; they were merchants on the mighty waters,' (Psalm 107:23)

RMS *Titanic* before she was painted, and before the promenade on the A-deck was enclosed

S hips had been crossing the Atlantic for centuries. Their number was substantially increased by the trade in slaves, many of whom suffered appallingly during the journey.

Chapter 2

Floating coffins

In 1819 the crossing of the first steam-assisted passenger ship took place. In the early days, the crossings were often extremely rough and conditions on board were primitive. There was no running water; there were no toilets; and there was no way to keep the food fresh once the supply of ice had melted. They did occasionally have fresh milk, which was supplied by an unfortunate sea-going cow. This poor animal was usually kept in what can only be described as a padded cell on deck. George Whitfield, the great eighteenth-century preacher, crossed the Atlantic thirteen times.

Charles Dickens and his wife made the crossing in 1842. He stated that it was like being in a 'profoundly preposterous box'. He also described the sleeping berths in this way: 'Nothing smaller for sleeping was ever made except coffins.'[1] Being a famous writer of his time, his musings on the subject naturally prejudiced people's thinking about crossing the Atlantic for many years.

It was not just the wealthy, however, that travelled across the Atlantic. Many immigrants made the crossing, especially since America had adopted the poem *The New Colossus* as part of its immigration statement—'Give me your tired, your poor, your huddled masses.'[2] These steerage, or third-class, passengers, became the 'bread and butter' of the cruise lines. Their travelling conditions were even worse than those referred to by Dickens, with no comforts at all and very little food. Often ships were referred to as 'floating coffins'.

Luxury

However, things did gradually improve. In 1850 the RMS *Atlantic* was launched. It had the addition of a drawing room and a separate dining room. There were even bathrooms and a barber shop, a vast improvement on what had gone before. From that time, every new ship that appeared seemed to bring with it some new luxury: bigger staterooms, electric lights, and hot and cold running water. The Germans were the first to give architects the task of designing the interiors. The SS *Amerika* launched in 1905 became literally a floating hotel with its own Ritz café. The Germans quickly cornered the market, building each ship bigger and better than the last.

There were, however, two rival companies in the race not only to attract passengers for the Atlantic crossing but also to win the unofficial accolade, the Blue Riband—the then non-existent trophy for the fastest crossing. These two companies were the American White Star Line and the British-American Cunard Line.

Cunard

Born in Nova Scotia, Samuel Cunard, who was a successful businessman, bid for and won the first contract to transport mail from Britain to North America in 1839. The following year, he set up the British and North American Royal Mail Steam Packet Company. Privately owned, it was reorganized as a public stock company in 1879 in order to raise more capital. It was then that it became known as the Cunard Steamship Company Ltd.

White Star Line

In 1867 Thomas Henry Ismay bought the then bankrupt White Star Line for the sum of £1,000 ($5,000). This deal was backed by Gustav Schwabe, a Liverpool financier, who agreed to it on the condition that White Star would purchase ships made by Harland & Wolff, a company owned by his nephew. In 1891 Thomas Ismay retired and passed the business on to his sons, Bruce and James Ismay. In 1902 IMM (International Mercantile Marine Company), owned by the American, J. Pierpont Morgan, bought the company for £10,000,000 ($50,000,000). Bruce Ismay was kept on in his position as Managing Director. William J. Pirrie, Managing Director and controlling Chairman of Harland & Wolff, joined Morgan and Ismay too.

In 1906, a loan from the British Government enabled Cunard to launch its two sister ships, RMS *Mauretania* and RMS *Lusitania*. They were powered by turbine engines and boasted the best first-class passenger appointments afloat. As a response to this, White Star Line owners, J. P. Morgan and J. Bruce Ismay, approached their favoured shipbuilder, Harland & Wolff, based in Belfast, with a view to building a new 'super liner'. Under the oversight of Lord Pirrie and his nephew, Thomas Andrews, plans were drawn up for the 'olympic' class ship. There would be three ships to begin with: the *Olympic*, the *Titanic* and the *Gigantic*, later renamed the *Britannic*. They were to be bigger and better than anything that had gone before.

Knocking off at Harland & Wolff, Belfast (showing the *Titanic* under construction in the background)

The shipyard had to be reorganized. Many more workers had to be employed. A specially constructed gantry had to be built. Designed by Sir William Arroll—famous for the construction of the Forth Bridge—the gantry covered an area of 840 by 240 feet, with a crane towering 214 feet overhead. Belfast had never seen anything like this before; the huge gantry towered over the skyline.

The keel for the *Olympic* was laid on the 16 December 1908 and fewer than fifteen weeks later the keel for the *Titanic* was laid on the 31 March 1909. Quality was certainly not compromised for speed as the best materials and designs were used, exceeding any regulations then in effect. Steel plates were riveted together using hydraulic equipment, ensuring better plating work than would have been achieved by conventional methods. In later investigations, the construction would be called to account as a possible factor in the sinking.

It is ironic that early in 1910 when the *Titanic* was being constructed, the fatal iceberg broke away and started its slow journey south towards the shipping lanes. Controlled by strong currents, it first travelled north around Baffin Bay before floating south towards the island of Newfoundland and the heavily trafficked shipping lanes.

On 20 October 1910, RMS *Olympic* was launched. There was no official launch party, no bottle of champagne swung against the prow of the ship, no person of note to declare, 'I name this ship …' It would be just the same for her sister ship, *Titanic*, seven months later on 31 May 1911.

Unsinkable?

It was a clear, bright beautiful May morning when Lord Pirrie and J. Bruce Ismay, along with other invited guests and members of the press, stood on specially constructed stands at Harland & Wolff to watch the launching of the *Titanic*. For workers at the shipyard, however, there would be no such luxury: they stood or sat where they could, but, at least, they did not have to pay for the privilege.

At that time, the *Titanic* was the largest man-made object ever to be moved. It was 882.8 feet long (268m) and 92.5 feet wide (28m). By comparison, Noah's Ark was 450 feet long (148m) and 75 feet wide (23m) and 45 feet high (13.5m). Stood on her end, the *Titanic* was almost twice as tall as the Great Pyramid of Khufu (Cheops in Greek) on the Giza plateau, and over twice as tall as St Peter's Cathedral in Rome.

More than 22 tons of tallow, soap and engine oil were used to grease the slipway to ensure the vessel's momentum, and three anchors and over 160 tons of drag cable were used to slow her down. As the final wooden shore under the bilge was knocked away only hydraulic triggers held the 46,328 ton ship. A red rocket was fired to warn all ships in the area to stay clear. At thirteen minutes past twelve, the triggers were released and the *Titanic* slid quietly down the greased slipway to the cheers of the onlookers.

A comparison between the size of RMS *Titanic's* propeller and the yard workers

James Dobbins was one of the many workers whose job that day was to knock away the wooden shores. Unfortunately, his leg was badly crushed by one of the shores and he was taken to hospital where, sadly, he died later that day from his injuries. He was not the first fatality on this project. On 20 April 1910, Samuel Joseph Scott, a rivet catcher, was working with one of the riveting crews when he fell from a ladder and fractured his skull. It was his job to place the glowing hot rivet into a hole where it would be riveted and then to be ready to receive (catch) the next one. He was just fifteen years old. On 30 July 2011, a headstone was placed on his unmarked grave in Belfast City Cemetery. In total there would be eight deaths registered at Harland & Wolff during the construction and fitting of the *Titanic*. For those days, without Health and Safety regulations, this was not a bad record.

Outfitting

The *Titanic* was launched, but that was only half the job done. She was next taken into dry dock where work began on the outfitting of the ship. A whole army of electricians, plumbers, carpenters, painters and decorators now assembled to bring her to completion. There were beautifully appointed first-class staterooms, with oak panelling in the sitting rooms, marble fireplaces, brass beds and private bathrooms. Even in the first class, it was an innovation to have an en-suite bathroom! In all, there would be 416 first-class cabins and staterooms. There was a covered promenade, elevators operating between decks, Turkish baths, a gymnasium, a squash court, a heated indoor swimming pool (the first of its kind), two cafés as well as the main dining room, a hospital and two barber shops. There was even a special dining room for the maids and valets of the rich and famous.

Perhaps the *Titanic's* grandest feature was the two main oak-panelled staircases. There was one aft and an even grander one forward: a huge, ornate staircase, with bronze cherubic statues, a large clock, and, most impressive of all, a luminous glass dome. First-class passengers would don their finest apparel and parade down the staircase for dinner.

Second-class passengers would not be disappointed. They had 162 cabins, their own dining room and smoking room, a library and, for the first time, their own elevator. It was generally thought that second-class accommodation aboard the *Titanic* rivalled first class on any other ship.

Third-class passengers were to be housed in 262 cabins, as well as in an open berthing area which accommodated forty beds. There were showers, a third-class dining room, and a piano in the saloon/common room. This was veritable luxury.

Next the superstructure was added. There was not enough room within the gantry to perform this task. The superstructure included the officers' quarters, the captain's cabin, and the bridge. Another important part of the superstructure was the Marconi office. Located on the boat deck, it would play a vital role on the night of the sinking. The distinctive four smoke stacks or funnels were now put in place. Three of these were chimneys to draw the smoke and soot away from the massive boiler rooms. The fourth funnel was, in fact, a dummy funnel as White Star, like a lot of companies at that time, considered that four funnels would give the ship a sleeker look.

At this stage, the three propellers were installed: the smaller middle propeller weighed in at a mighty 22 tons, while the outer two weighed 38 tons each. The *Titanic* would also have three anchors, the largest being over 18 feet long and weighing over 14 tons. They had to be pulled through the streets on the back of a cart by twenty horses. A single link in the anchor chain weighed in at a massive 175 pounds (79 kg).

In June 1911, in a special edition devoted to the *Titanic* and the *Olympic*, the trade journal *The Shipbuilder and Marine Engine Builder* stated: 'The Captain may, by simply moving an electric switch, instantly close the watertight doors throughout, making the vessel virtually unsinkable.'[3]

Lifeboats

It was also during the fitting that the lifeboats were added. The British Board of Trade, which regulated the safety of all shipping, stipulated that ships should be able to accommodate 1060 people in lifeboats, which meant that the *Titanic* needed only sixteen lifeboats. This ruling was introduced in 1896 when ships did not exceed 10,000 tons. However, ocean liners had more than quadrupled in size with the *Titanic* weighing over 46,000 tons, making the ruling woefully out of date. The *Titanic* was actually fitted with sixteen lifeboats and four Englehardt collapsibles which could accommodate 1178 persons. The *Titanic's* total capacity, crew and passengers, could exceed 3,500.

History has proved that Alexander Carlisle, who was one of the managing directors at Harland & Wolff, actually planned that the *Titanic* should accommodate at least sixty-four lifeboats. He had persuaded the company to install the new Welin davit in order to facilitate this. This number would later be reduced to thirty-two and finally to sixteen. White Star had agreed to the new davits but considered that thirty-two lifeboats would be too expensive and would unsettle the passengers and make them doubt the soundness of the ship.

A provisional date of 20 March 1912 was given for the maiden voyage, but on 20 September 1911, the *Olympic*, outward-bound from Southampton with Captain Edward J. Smith at the helm, collided with the British Royal Navy cruiser, *Hawke*. Both ships were badly damaged. In the inquiry that followed, blame fell on the *Olympic*. The Navy claimed that her sheer size and displacement had caused the *Hawke* to be sucked into the path of the liner. (HMS *Hawke* would be torpedoed and sunk early in World War I.)

Although she now had a gaping hole in her starboard (right) side, the *Olympic* was still able to limp back to dry dock in Belfast by 6 October. However, as workers now had to be diverted to repairing the *Olympic*, the *Titanic's* maiden voyage was delayed until 10 April 1912.

Sea Trials

The fitting of the *Titanic* having been finally completed, it would now be the time to begin the tests to see if she was seaworthy. These were scheduled for the first two days of April but owing to bad weather did not start until 6.00 a.m. on the 2 April, only eight days before the scheduled maiden voyage. On board was a work gang—seventy-eight men in total—of stokers, engineers, electricians, firemen, greasers, as well as two Marconi officers. Thomas Andrews (for Harland & Wolff) and several members of the crew, together with the ship's officers and Captain Smith, were also there.

In just one day, the ship was put through her paces: speed trails and manoeuvrability. At about 2.00 p.m. the *Titanic* briefly reached a speed of 21 knots (approx. 24 mph—her top speed was 23/24 knots) and by 8.00 p.m. the trials were over. What was not noted by the Board of Trade inspector, or, at least, it was not mentioned in the report, was that a fire was burning in one of the coal bunkers which fed boiler room 6. The papers were signed and the *Titanic* was ready to set sail for Southampton and destiny.

Notes

1 **Ballard, Dr Robert D.,** and **Archbold, Rick,** *Lost Liners* (Toronto: Madison Press Books, 1987) 16

2 *The New Colossus,* a poem by **Emma Lazarus** written in 1883, engraved on a bronze plaque and placed inside the Statue of Liberty in 1903. www.libertystatepark.com/emma.htm

3 *The Shipbuilder and Marine Engine Builder,* a trade journal which had as a special feature articles on the *Olympic* and the *Titanic* in its June 1911 edition. www.the-titanic.co.uk/the-titanic.htm

Maiden Voyage

'Although they are so large and are driven by strong winds, they are steered by a very small rudder wherever the pilot wants to go,' (James 3:4).

RMS *Titanic* at Southampton Docks prior to sailing for New York

Chapter 3

T he excitement was mounting, as the world's most luxurious ship underwent the final preparations for her maiden voyage. Many of the world's rich and famous were going to experience the voyage of their lives.

Southampton

It was a bright and breezy Wednesday morning on the 10 April 1912. Crew members had been arriving since sunrise, walking up the gangways to find their cabins and stow their gear. Stewards, stewardesses, elevator operators, chefs, waiters, barbers, gym instructor, butchers, bakers, squash court attendants all came. In fact, everyone this floating hotel would need to help her run smoothly was there. Band leader, Wallace Hartley, and his fellow musicians also arrived bringing with them the latest music to entertain the passengers. Also boarding were the 'unseen' engineers, electricians, stokers and firemen who would work in the deep bowels of the ship making sure that the mighty *Titanic* would reach her destination.

Harland & Wolff employees, making up a 'guarantee group', were also on board, joined by Thomas Andrews, the shipbuilder. As was the custom, they would accompany the ship on her maiden voyage to iron out any 'bugs'. While Andrews had first-class accommodation, the rest of the group travelled as second-class passengers. The officers had spent the night on board. They were familiarizing themselves with this giant of a ship, while awaiting the arrival of the captain.

The Officers

These were the officers on board the *Titanic*:

Chief Officer: Henry Tingle Wilde
First Officer: William McMaster Murdoch
Second Officer: Charles Herbert Lightoller
Third Officer: Herbert John Pitman

Fourth Officer: Joseph Groves Boxhall
Fifth Officer: Harold Godfrey Lowe
Sixth Officer: James Paul Moody
All but one of the officers had been aboard the ship during her sea trials. Originally, William Murdoch was to be her Chief Officer, but a last-minute 'officer reshuffle' saw Henry Wilde transfer from the *Olympic* and join the crew of the *Titanic* at Southampton as her new Chief Officer, second only to the captain. This change would result in Murdoch and Lightoller being demoted and would exclude the original Second Officer, David Blair, altogether.

Captain Edward John Smith

At 7.00 a.m. Captain Edward John Smith arrived. He cut quite a figure with his white hair and neatly trimmed white beard and moustache (looking not unlike Captain Birdseye in the British Television advertisements). Born in Stoke-on-Trent in 1850, a White Star employee since 1880 and a captain since 1887, it would fall to him to lead the *Titanic* out on her maiden voyage. Soon to retire, this captain, aged sixty-two, was a popular choice among the crew and, more particularly, the passengers. Nicknamed 'the Millionaire's Captain', he was often the favoured choice of the rich and

Captain Smith of RMS *Titanic*. This photo appeared in the *New York Times* some days after his death

famous. Despite the incident a few months earlier involving HMS *Hawke*, the company seemed to have every faith in him.

Passengers

Shortly before 9.30 a.m. passengers began to board. Embarking through an entrance near the stern on C deck, were the third-class passengers. There, medical officers scanned them, a cursory look at British subjects but a more thorough inspection was given to all 'foreign' passengers. Cabins were located on the lower accommodation decks (D, E, F and G) and usually forward or aft. Prices for a third-class single trip usually started at about £7/£8 ($35/$40) and did include all meals on board.

To put this into perspective, the average salary in 1912 for an Irish farmer was 8 pence per day. In those days, there were 240 pennies to the pound. Therefore, it would have taken approximately nine months' salary to pay for a single ticket on board the *Titanic*. The average Welsh miner earned £82 per year and the average American wage was $750 per year. The exchange rate in those days was £1.00/$5.00.

Second-class passengers also boarded through C deck, although they were brought through their own entrance slightly further forward of the third-class entrance. They were then escorted by stewards along the hallway or taken in the elevator to their cabins, which were also located on D, E and F decks, but slightly further forward. Prices for second-class tickets started at £10 ($50), usually in shared accommodation, but some passengers paid as much as £74 ($370) for the privilege of a private room.

First-class passengers embarked through the main entrance on B deck, where they were greeted by Chief Steward Latimer and his staff. From there, they and any staff travelling with them were gently escorted down the corridors of A, B, C and D deck to their staterooms or cabins. Ticket prices would vary from £26 ($150) for a basic cabin to £870 ($4,350) for a stateroom.

Once the passengers were all safely on board, the ship's officers took up their respective positions. At about 12 noon, the *Titanic* gently slipped her moorings and, as the tugs took up the slack, slowly reversed away from the dock out into the River Test. The passengers leaned over the port side and, to the sound of cheers and whistles, waved their goodbyes to loved ones.

In Control

On the bridge were Captain Smith and Harbour Pilot, George Bowyer. Under their supervision, the *Titanic* turned slowly to port and completed her turn. The order *ahead slow* was given. Her mighty propellers began to cut through the water, as the tugs began to slacken off. As she began to pick up speed, a tremendous wake, caused by the turning of her huge screws and by the narrow passage of the river channel, caused another nearby liner, the SS *New York*, to snap her mooring ropes. As the *New York* began to drift dangerously in the direction of the *Titanic*, the quick-thinking Captain Gale of the tug *Vulcan* commanded his men to get a rope on to her. Meanwhile, on the *Titanic*, Captain Smith and Pilot Bowyer gave the order *full astern*. Finally, with the SS *New York* now only four feet away from the *Titanic*, the *Vulcan* managed to get a line on her and pull her to safety.

One must wonder what was going through the minds of Captain Smith and Pilot Bowyer, both of whom had been on the bridge of the *Olympic* when she collided with HMS *Hawke* only a few months earlier. In 1907 Captain Smith had been quoted as saying, 'When anyone asks me how I can best describe my experiences of nearly forty years at sea, I merely say "uneventful". I have never been in an accident of any sort worth speaking about. I never saw a wreck and have never been wrecked, nor was I ever in any predicament that threatened to end in disaster of any sort.'[1] Whatever they were thinking at that moment, they had had a narrow escape.

With the SS *New York* being towed to a new mooring, the *Titanic* was able to start her voyage out into the Solent a second time, stopping briefly to drop off Bowyer near the Nab Light Vessel, and then sailing out into the Channel.

Cherbourg

Although Cherbourg was a deep-water port, it did not have a dock suitable for a large vessel such as the *Titanic*. So passengers were ferried out on two White Star tenders, the *Nomadic* (used for first and second-class passengers) and the *Traffic* (used for third-class passengers and conveyance of mail). At 6.30 p.m. the *Titanic* finally dropped anchor, her arrival being delayed because of the incident at Southampton. Twenty-two passengers would be disembarking and 274 passengers would be coming on board. Among these were 102 third-class passengers including a large group of 'Continentals' from Syria, Croatia, Armenia and other countries in the Middle East who had been re-routed through Paris and then on to Cherbourg. They considered themselves fortunate to be sailing on the new, elegant *Titanic*.

At 8.00 p.m., only an hour and a half later, all passengers, cargo and mail had been transferred and the *Titanic* was once again under way.

Queenstown (now Cobh, Cork)

As the *Titanic* continued her journey to Ireland, passengers had a chance to explore this mighty vessel and to sample the delights she had to offer. They would also be spending their first night afloat. At 7.30 p.m. P. W. Fletcher, the ship's bugler, went from deck to deck summoning first-class passengers to dinner in their elegant Dining Room. Although we do not know what they ate that first night on board, it is likely to have been a sumptuous affair, consisting of at least ten courses. Meals for the second class were prepared in the same kitchen and, though not as lavish, would still have been a sight to behold.

The catering staff certainly had a lot to choose from: 11,000lb (4990 kg) of fresh fish, 75,000lb (34020 kg) of fresh meat, 7,500lb (3402 kg) of bacon and ham, 25,000lb (11340 kg) of poultry and game, and 40 tons of potatoes. There were also 40,000 fresh eggs and 200 barrels of flour, not to mention grapes, oranges and lemons. The list of provisions was endless.

Passengers in the third class were given 'plain food', something like soup, corned beef and cabbage with boiled potatoes, followed by peaches and rice. This menu was taken from a White Star Line specimen menu. Their palate was not considered to be as refined as that of the passengers in first and second class. Still this menu was a great deal better than would have been the norm for the day. Until recently, passengers had had to supply their own food on sea voyages!

Thursday morning was bright but a little breezy. To many on board the ship, though, the *Titanic* seemed very 'steady'. At 11.30 a.m. she dropped anchor off the coast of Ireland. The tenders *America* and *Ireland* ferried out 120 more passengers and 1,385 sacks of mail.

Among the passengers disembarking was thirty-one-year-old Francis M. Browne, a teacher in Dublin and a novitiate for the priesthood, which he would join in 1915. Travelling first class, he had brought with him a special gift from his uncle, a camera. While on board, he took several photos which would become known as the 'Father Browne Photos'. These would be shown worldwide after the sinking.

Also disembarking was John Coffey, a twenty-four-year-old stoker. Joining the ship in Southampton, he was listed as AWOL (Absent Without Leave) after docking in Queenstown where he lived. It is likely that he joined the ship only for the purpose of crossing the channel. Possibly, he hid among the mail bags intended for Ireland.

Finally, at 1.30 p.m. the *Titanic* weighed anchor and executed a turn to starboard. She thus began her last journey towards the Atlantic and New York. On board one of the tenders, Francis Browne raised his camera and took one last photo as, cheered on by local fishermen, the *Titanic* left the Irish coast behind her.

Note

1   **Lord, Walter,** *The Night Lives On* (Middlesex, England: Viking, 1987) 39

Atlantic Crossing

'The sea is his, for he made it,' (Psalm 95:5).

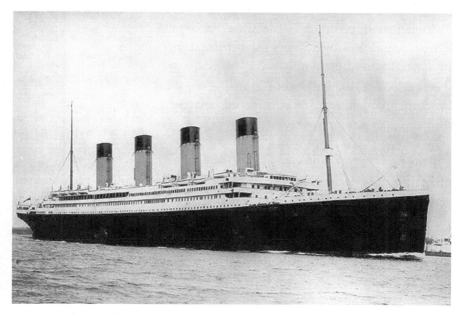

RMS *Titanic* departing from Southampton on 10 April 1912

O ver the next few days, the 1,300 passengers began to settle into life at sea. The ocean was remarkably calm but the weather began to get progressively colder.

Life on the ocean wave

For those travelling in first class, there were a few diversions. For example, for the more athletic, there were the Turkish or electric baths on F deck, the indoor swimming pool (which was filled with sea water and slightly heated), a session on the squash court, or a workout in the gymnasium. For those who preferred a more sedate life, there was the library on A deck, or the à la carte restaurant known affectionately as 'The Ritz'. It was also known as the Veranda/Palm Court Café. As an alternative, located just opposite was the Café Parisien. There were, however, very few formal or organized activities. There were no balls or dances. In fact, the highlight of the day would be dinner which was usually served between 6.00 and 7.30 p.m.

In the gymnasium: a female passenger (unknown) and Mr Lawrence Beesley

Wireless

One of the 'fads' in which the first-class passengers could indulge was the recently invented Marconigram. Starting at 12 shillings ($3)—in today's money, 60 pence (90 cents)—they could send a message to friends or loved ones. The Marconi Wireless (Radio Telegraph System) was invented by the Italian, Guglielmo Marconi, in the late 1890s. By 1912 most passenger liners were fitted with wireless as standard equipment. This system had proved its worth in 1909 when the operator, Jack Binns, signalled for help. His ship, the RMS *Republic*, (White Star Line) had collided in thick fog with the SS *Florida*. His ceaseless efforts in sending out messages for help meant that all passengers and crew were rescued. There were seven fatalities on board the SS *Florida* caused by the impact.

Normally ships would have only one wireless operator who would work a fourteen-hour shift, switching off the equipment when he retired. The *Titanic* had two operators on board: twenty-five-year-old John George 'Jack' Phillips and twenty-two-year-old Harold Sydney Bride. This meant that the *Titanic* could transmit twenty-four hours a day. Strangely enough, Bride and Phillips were employed by both White Star Line and Marconi. Bride stated at the inquiry that he was paid £2 5s ($12) a month by White Star and £4 ($20) by Marconi. As senior operator, Phillips would no doubt have earned slightly more.

First-class passengers could also join a sweepstake to see how far the *Titanic* had travelled in a twenty-four-hour period. From 12 noon on Thursday to 12 noon on Friday, she had covered 386 miles. From Friday to Saturday, she covered 519 miles and from Saturday to Sunday, 546 miles. The *Titanic* was increasing her speed.

Wallace Hartley

Music was one of the few pleasures on board enjoyed by both first and second class. The band leader, Wallace Hartley, had a group of seven musicians working for him. He would play in a quintet. A trio would play in the Café Parisien. They were employed by a music agency and not by White Star Line. Therefore, they had to pay for their uniforms and their passage from their earnings. Only Hartley, as bandleader, was offered second-class accommodation free of charge.

There was also an opportunity for some good socializing. The first-class passenger list read as a veritable Who's Who afloat. Perhaps the most notable names on this list were John Jacob Astor IV and his new wife, Madeline. Mr Astor was the grandson of John Jacob Astor I, who had made his fortune in opium, fur and the real estate business and had founded one of the wealthiest families in the US. However, in spite of his great wealth, John Astor IV had found himself shunned by the elite society he enjoyed when he divorced his wife in 1909. Divorce was a rare occurrence in the early 1900s. When the forty-seven-year-old married eighteen-year-old Madeline Talmage Force, the couple felt compelled to go on an 'extended' honeymoon in the hopes that the scandal would die down. One of the few socialites who did not shun them was Margaret Brown. She happened to be returning home on the same voyage. Margaret would later become known as 'The Unsinkable Molly Brown'. Born in Missouri to poor Irish immigrant parents, her background could

Rev. John Harper pictured here with his daughter, aged six

not have been more different from that of John Jacob Astor. In 1894 her husband had 'struck it rich' when an ore seam was discovered in a mine in which he had shares.

Also travelling back to New York were Mr and Mrs Isidor Straus. Mr Straus was a German Jew who had moved to America in 1854. In 1865, at the age of twenty, he and his brother had set up a crockery and glassware business inside the R. H. Macy & Co. Department Store. Less than thirty years later, they became the owners of that store. The Strauses, both in their late sixties, were a devoted couple and were often seen walking hand in hand, a regular 'Darby and Joan'.

Other notables on board were: Major Archibald Butt, military aide to President Taft; Mr and Mrs Charles Melville Hays, Mr Hays was President of the Grand Trunk Railroad in America; Sir Cosmo Duff Gordon, known as a sherry producer, he had fenced for Great Britain in the 1909 Olympics, and his wife, Lady Duff Gordon, a leading fashion designer. Colonel Archibald Gracie, author and amateur historian, was also making the trip.

John Harper

Not as noteworthy, perhaps, from the world's point of view, was Rev. John Harper. He embarked at Southampton on Wednesday 10 April and travelled second class, on ticket number 248727 that cost £33 ($165). Rev. Harper, a man of thirty-nine years and a widower, was the pastor of the Memorial Baptist Church in Glasgow. En route to Chicago with his six-year-old daughter, Annie Jessie Harper (known as Nina), and his niece, Jessie Wills Leitch, who was Annie's nanny, he was planning to lead a series of revival meetings at the Moody Church in that great city.

Born in 1872 in Houston, Renfrewshire in Scotland, he had come to faith in Christ at the age of thirteen and by the age of eighteen had begun to preach on the street corner of his local village in the evening, while working in the mill during the day. Six years later, he was offered his first full-time ministry in Govan, near Glasgow.

It is perhaps worth noting that at the age of two and half, John Harper fell down a well and had to be resuscitated. Then, at the age of twenty-six, he was swept out to sea by a reverse current—an incident he barely survived. At the age of thirty-two, he found himself on a leaking ship in the Mediterranean. Rev. Harper and water did not go well together!

His brother, George Harper, was also a minister of the gospel, serving at Gorgie Baptist Church, Edinburgh which is, sadly, no longer in existence. From 1921 to 1927, he was pastor at Lansdowne Hall West Norwood (later known as Lansdowne Evangelical Free Church), where he followed the founding pastor, William Fuller Gooch. A member of the church was E. J. Poole-Connor, one of the founders of the Fellowship of Independent Evangelical Churches (FIEC). Poole-Connor was buried in West Norwood cemetery not far from the grave of C. H. Spurgeon, (for details see *Travel with C. H. Spurgeon,* published by Day One Publications, 2002.)

William T. Stead

Stead was a crusading journalist and the editor of the influential *Pall Mall Gazette*—a newspaper which took up the cause of victims.

In February 1885, Annie Swan, a seventeen-year-old girl, was found huddled on the doorstep of the Salvation Army's Headquarters in Queen Victoria Street. She had gone to London from Sussex in response to an advertisement for domestic staff. When she got there, she found that she had been lured into the savage clutches of a brothel keeper. Having managed to make her escape, she sought refuge at the Salvation Army which she considered to be the only place where she could find help. Bramwell Booth was shocked by her story, and also by the fact that many younger girls were being held as virtual slaves to satisfy the lusts of the rich clientele.

William T. Stead agreed to investigate this sordid situation. Along with some others, he set out to discover the extent of the horrific trade in young girls. The legal age of consent was thirteen, but many of those involved could not produce a birth certificate to confirm their age. This, of course, was much to the delight of the predatory classes.

Through Stead's heroic endeavours, Parliament passed the Criminal Amendment Act, which raised the age of consent from thirteen to sixteen years of age.

(For further information see *Travel with William Booth*, published by Day One Publications, 2003.)

The *Titanic* was a floating microcosm of people from all walks of life: Catholic, Protestant, Salvation Army, Muslim, and many more. There were rich, poor, young, old, newlyweds, adulterers, gamblers, drunkards and teetotallers. The whole world seemed to be present on the *Titanic*.

A night to remember

'Man proposes but God disposes.' (Thomas À Kempis)[1]

The Grand Staircase on the *Titanic's* sister ship, RMS *Olympic*

Sunday morning 14 April 1912 dawned cold and bright with a slight, but bracing, breeze. It was so cold that most passengers chose to stay in the common room rather than to go and sit or stroll on the deck. The sea was like a millpond, so still there was hardly a ripple.

Lifeboat drill, not required

News had come through from boiler room 6 that the coalbunker fire had been extinguished during Saturday evening. Speculation as to whether the fire played a part in the *Titanic's* sinking by weakening her bulkheads has raged ever since.

In any normal year, the route the *Titanic* was taking would have kept her clear from icebergs. But this was an unusual year. 48° North is the key line for iceberg danger. For some years, no bergs had appeared, but 1912 was to prove to be an exceptional year. Over three hundred icebergs crossed this critical line as the Labrador Current flowed unusually southward.

In turn, this pushed the warmer Gulf Stream south so that the icebergs did not melt where they would normally have done so.

It was the practice of White Star Line to have a lifeboat drill on a Sunday morning, involving all passengers and crew. For some reason, Captain Smith decided to cancel it. There have been a lot of theories put forward over the years as to why he did this. One is that he thought no one would attend as it was so cold. Another is that he did not want to draw attention to the fact there was not enough room in the boats for everyone. We will never know for certain what his reasons were.

Prayer for those in peril on the sea

At 10.00 a.m. there was a Sunday morning service held in the First Class Dining Saloon, which Captain Smith himself led. Colonel Gracie would later state: 'I was very much impressed with the "Prayer for those at Sea".'[2] The service ended with the gathered passengers singing *Our God, our help in ages past*. It was probably one of the few occasions when passengers from all three classes would join together.

At 1.42 p.m. an ice warning was received from the SS *Baltic* and delivered to Captain Smith on the bridge. During a conversation with Bruce Ismay, Smith showed him the message, which, astonishingly, was pocketed by Ismay who then showed it to some of his fellow passengers. This was possibly an opportunity for him to demonstrate his importance. It was not until 7.15 p.m. that Captain Smith retrieved the message from Ismay and posted it in the chart room. This event, along with several others, has caused people to question who was really in charge—the captain or the owner. In the afternoon, twenty-four of the twenty-nine ship's boilers were lit and the ship reached a speed of 20.5 knots. The plan was to light the rest of the boilers on Monday, thereby working the *Titanic* up to her full speed.

At 5.30 p.m. the *Titanic* changed direction. By making this decision, Captain Smith unknowingly brought the ship on to a collision course with the iceberg. The ship steaming at a speed of 21.5 knots on a flat, calm sea, and on a night with no moon would prove to be disastrous.

Wealthy passengers, Mr and Mrs George Widener, held a private dinner in the à la carte restaurant at 7.30 p.m. Mr Widener was a hotel owner and a streetcar magnate. Captain Smith, who was the guest of honour, attended the party.

At this time a message, warning of ice in the area, was received from the SS *Californian* and was delivered to the bridge. This message was not seen by Captain Smith or Bruce Ismay.

In the evening, second-class passenger, Rev. Ernest Courtenay Carter, arranged with the purser to hold a 'Hymn Service' from 8.30 p.m. until 10.00 p.m. The service was attended by about one hundred passengers. Before the singing of each hymn, Rev. Carter gave a brief account of its history and author. Lawrence Beesley, a teacher, who survived the sinking, reported this item.

There may be trouble ahead

Just before 9.00 p.m., Captain Smith excused himself from the party and went up to the bridge where Second Officer Charles Lightoller was on duty. After a brief conversation about the weather, Captain Smith retired for the evening. His parting words were, 'If it becomes at all doubtful, let me know at once. I shall be just inside.'[3] At 9.40 p.m. Harold Bride, Marconi operator, turned in for the night, leaving his colleague, Jack Phillips, on duty.

It is known that the SS *Mesaba* sent a wireless message to the *Titanic* to warn her of 'heavy pack ice and large icebergs' at this time. There is no record of this message ever going up to the bridge. The wireless set had broken down the day before, that is, on Saturday, and Phillips and Bride had worked for hours repairing it. Phillips would have been extremely busy catching up with the day's commercial traffic and it is likely that this ice warning was just buried under all the other messages. The *Titanic* had received a number of iceberg warnings that day from several different ships travelling through the same area but, even though all of them except the *Mesaba's* message had made it to the chart room, not all of them were plotted.

At 10.00 p.m., up in the crow's nest, lookouts, Reginald Lee and Frederick Fleet, began their watch for the night. They had been told to 'keep a sharp lookout for ice, particularly small ice and growlers'.[4] Their job was made all the harder by the flat, calm surface of the sea which would mean that there would be no ripples to signify breakers at the base of an iceberg. It was also made difficult by the fact that they had not been equipped with glasses (binoculars), in spite of their numerous requests for them since leaving Southampton.

At this time, too, Lightoller was relieved on the bridge by First Officer William Murdoch. Lightoller made his final round of the ship, reminding the ship's carpenter, J. Maxwell, to look after the fresh water supply as it was likely to freeze. He then retired to his cabin.

At 10.55 p.m., the SS *Californian*, under the command of Captain Lord, had come to a complete stop because of the ice. Its wireless operator, Cyril Evans, had tried to contact the *Titanic* to warn her of the proximity of ice but he was told, 'Keep out! Shut up! I'm working Cape

Race's[5] by a rather beleaguered Phillips. Evans listened to the *Titanic's* transmissions for a further twenty minutes before turning off his Marconi set and going to bed.

Key, what key?

In 2005 newspapers ran a story regarding a locker key from the *Titanic* which was up for auction. The locker key was in the possession of David Blair, who had been displaced as Second Officer in the reshuffle. Apparently, in his haste to leave, he had forgotten to hand over the key to Second Officer Lightoller. It was suggested that the locker in question held the aforementioned glasses which may have made the difference between safety and disaster on that fatal night.

Notes

1 à Kempis, Thomas, *The Imitation of Christ*, Book i, Chapter 19 (New York: P.F. Collier and Son Company, 1909)

2 Gracie, Colonel Archibald, *Titanic: A Survivor's Story* (London: Alan Sutton Publishers Ltd, 1985) 8

3 Eaton, John P., and Haas, Charles A., *Titanic: Triumph and Tragedy* (Wellingborough, Northamptonshire, England: Patrick Stephens Ltd, 1987) 115

4 Eaton, John P., and Haas, Charles A., *Titanic: Triumph and Tragedy* (Wellingborough, Northamptonshire, England: Patrick Stephens Ltd, 1987) 115

5 Eaton, John P., and Haas, Charles A., *Titanic: Triumph and Tragedy* (Wellingborough, Northamptonshire, England: Patrick Stephens Ltd, 1987) 115

What did you see?

'The ship struck a sandbar and ran aground. The bow stuck fast and would not move, and the stern was broken to pieces by the pounding of the surf,' (Acts 27:41).

A sepia picture of the suspect iceberg was one of a series taken by Stephan Rehorek, a Czech sailor on board the German passenger steamer, *Bremen*. It was going to New York, but was diverted to the disaster area on 20 April 1912, six days after the event. The crew was horrified to see more than 100 bodies of passengers and crew floating in the Atlantic

By 11.30 p.m. most of the passengers had retired to their cabins, leaving only a few strong-spirited individuals still up to hear the sound of the seven bells being rung on the bridge. A slight mist or haze now hung in the air as lookouts, Fleet and Lee, suspended 50 feet up in the crow's nest, strained to see what lay ahead. There was no moon that night, but the sky was emblazoned with stars. At 11.39 p.m. the berg was only 1,000 yards (914 metres) away but was still quite invisible to the naked eye.

Disaster looms

Quite suddenly, at about 11.40 p.m., something loomed large and dark ahead. Frederick Fleet rang the crow's nest bell three times and lifted the interconnecting phone, which would put him straight through to the bridge. After what seemed like a lifetime to Fleet, Sixth Officer Moody answered, 'What did you see?'

'Iceberg right ahead,' replied Fleet.

'Thank you,' came the amazingly calm reply.

First Officer Murdoch reacted swiftly, swinging the mighty ship into action, instructing Quartermaster Hichens, who was the helmsman at the wheel, to *hard-a-starboard*. He then rushed to the engine room telegraph and rang for *stop*, then *full speed astern* in an effort to slow her down. He also pushed the button on the panel near the helmsman to close the watertight doors.

Some assume that First Officer William Murdoch made a fatal mistake when the iceberg appeared directly in front of the ship. However, he decided to attempt to clear the berg by swinging the ship to its port side. He gave the order *hard-a-starboard*, which was a Tiller Order directing the helmsman to turn the wheel to port (anti-clockwise) as far as it would go. The introduction of the steering wheel did not replace the tiller. It simply allowed the steering position to be moved elsewhere in the ship. The cables from the wheel would still control the movement of the tiller. The officer was commanding the helmsman to perform a particular task (moving the tiller to starboard) which would have the effect that he wanted. The *Titanic's* steering gear then pushed the tiller towards the starboard side of the ship, swinging the rudder over to port and causing the vessel to turn to port. This seems confusing and contradictory today, but to generations of sailors trained on sailing vessels with tiller steering it seemed perfectly logical and was understood by all seafarers. Only after wheel-and-tiller steering had come into the industry and new generations of sailors had undergone training on ships on which this new system was used was tiller steering rendered obsolete.

View of the stern and tiller of the *Titanic* in dry dock

Up in the crow's nest, Fleet and Lee watched as the iceberg drew nearer. Only thirty-seven seconds had passed since Fleet made the call. But it seemed to them that the ship was not going to avoid a head-on collision. Then slowly, very slowly, the whole ship, vibrating under the pressure, began to turn to port. The steering mechanism of the day meant that turning the wheel to the right, that is, starboard, would make the ship go left, that is, port.

Another view of the iceberg suspected of having sunk RMS *Titanic*. The chief steward of the liner *Prinze Adelbert* photographed this iceberg on the morning of 15 April 1912, just a few miles south of where the *Titanic* went down. The steward had not yet heard about the *Titanic*. What caught his attention was the smear of red paint along the base of the berg, an indication that it had collided with a ship at sometime in the preceding twelve hours

It is not that impressive

Eyewitnesses said that the berg towered over 50 to 100 feet above the water. What could not be seen was what was hidden beneath the water. Icebergs show only one ninth of their size above water. According to Michael Davie's book *The Titanic—The Full Story of a Tragedy*, the Ice Patrol states that icebergs of approximately 50 feet usually weigh something in the region of 500,000 tons—almost the weight of a small island.

Although avoiding a direct collision, the riveted steel plates of the *Titanic* scraped along the hard ice. There has been a lot of debate over the years as to how the damage was inflicted. Did the berg have protrusions or diamond sharp fingers which penetrated the ship's metal plating or was she practically grounded upon the berg? Whichever way it happened, the *Titanic* was damaged along her starboard side. The impact, however, seemed unusually gentle and, in many parts of the ship, was not felt at all. Many passengers slept through the event. Indeed, up in the crow's nest, Fleet would later state that they had had 'a narrow shave'.[1] Nearly all the passengers seemed totally unaware that anything serious had taken place. The only visible sign was some ice that had fallen on to the Well Deck.

A different view of the iceberg suspected of having sunk RMS *Titanic*. This print was in the possession of Captain De Carteret, the Captain of the Cable ship *Minia*. He reportedly stated that this was the only iceberg near the scene of the collision. Comparison with the previous picture seems to show that this picture was taken from the other side of the berg. Notice the curve of ice on the left which seems to correspond to the curve of ice on the right in the previous picture.

A dreadful surprise

Down in the bowels of the ship it was a different story. Hidden from the eyes of the passengers, working in filthy, hot conditions was the 'black gang' (so called because they were usually black from soot and coal dust). They knew nothing of what was going on 'up top'. For the workers in the boiler and engine rooms, the first sign that there was any trouble, was the sound of the warning bell and the flashing red light which came on as the watertight doors began to close, separating the ship into sixteen watertight compartments. This was followed by the order to *shut the doors*, meaning that all furnace doors were to be shut. Then, suddenly, there was a crash.

A great finger of ice penetrated at least three feet into hold 1, causing freezing sea water to pour in. In boiler rooms 5 and 6, a steady stream of water gushed in at 400 cubic feet per minute (the equivalent of 12 tons of water per minute). Men in these rooms scrambled through watertight doors which were closing and hastened up stairwells in an effort to escape the bitterly cold water. They were called back later. Many of them had no idea what had happened.

What shall we do?

As Captain Smith appeared on the bridge, the vibrations alerted him to the fact that something was wrong with his ship. He gave the order to the helmsmen to *ahead slow*, then after two or three minutes to *stop*, bringing the *Titanic's* engines to a stop for the last time. After questioning Murdoch, he commanded Fourth Officer Boxhall to inspect the forward area below and report back. On the way, Boxhall alerted officers Lightoller and Pitman, telling them what had happened, and then reported back to the Captain. He could see no damage above F deck (seven decks down and three decks up from the keel), but reported that postal clerk, John Smith, had stated that five minutes after the crash, the postal officers were standing in water up to their knees and were trying to lift 200 mail sacks from the Orlop Deck (two decks below F) up into the mail room on the deck above.

Next to arrive on the bridge that night was Bruce Ismay, still dressed in his nightwear. He was asking about the *Titanic's* condition. The ship was silent now, her usual humming engines and gentle vibration no longer lulling the passengers to sleep. Slowly, people became aware that something was amiss. Boxhall was asked by the Captain to work out their position.

Captain Smith gave orders to awaken Thomas Andrews, the ship's designer. If anyone could know how serious the situation was, it was he. Andrews, however, was not asleep but examining the ship's blueprints and checking his notes for improvements to the ship. He was so lost in his work that he did not even notice that anything had happened. At 11.50 p.m. Andrews and Captain Smith took a tour of the ship to assess the damage, passing by some of the passengers who were now milling around on the deck. The news was not good. There was water in the forepeak, holds 1 and 2, the mail room and boiler rooms 5 and 6. The *Titanic* had been built to float with any four of her first five compartments flooded, but she could not survive with water entering all five. In order for a compartment to be 'watertight', the bulkheads had to ascend through all the decks. But the division or bulkheads between compartments 5 and 6 only went as high as E deck. This meant that water would reach the top of

5 and overflow into 6; and when it had reached the top of 6, it would flow over into 7 and so on, gradually pulling the ship down by the head.

Down in the boiler rooms, the order had gone out to *draw the fires*. In boiler room 6, all the firemen and stokers were now working waist-deep in the freezing water, drawing out the hot coals from the boilers to prevent them from exploding when the cold sea water hit them. In boiler room 5, a pump had been installed by some of the engineers and, for the moment, it seemed to be just about holding its own.

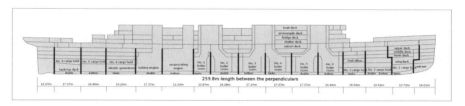

Cross section of the *Titanic*, showing the various compartments and levels

All is not well

Although only twenty minutes had elapsed since the impact, Captain Smith now knew that his ship was dying. Thomas Andrews advised Smith that the *Titanic* probably had only an hour or an hour and a half left to live. At just past midnight, Smith gave Chief Officer Wilde the instruction to uncover the lifeboats and First Officer Murdoch to alert the passengers. The level of shock that everyone on the bridge must have experienced at that moment can only be imagined. Although never actually called 'unsinkable', this ship had seemed so safe, so secure; every conceivable safety measure had been used in her construction. Suddenly, the cold night air was pierced with a shrill, deafening whistle. The pressure in the engines had been built up to propel the *Titanic* through the water, but now that she was at a standstill, the pressure had to be released. Steam was pouring out, activating the whistles attached to the funnels.

At this point, Captain Smith went to the wireless shack on the port side of the boat deck. Both Phillips and Bride were now on duty, Bride having decided to relieve Phillips early. Informing them of the situation and handing them details of their position, worked out by Boxhall as 41° 46' N, 50° 14' W, Captain Smith told them to send the call for assistance. These co-ordinates would be considered the official position of the *Titanic* for many years, but time has proved that they were, in fact, incorrect. Phillips immediately got on the set and tapped out the standard distress call CQD which was often thought to stand for 'Come Quick Danger but, in fact, held no significance at all other than being the normal distress call sign. He followed it with the *Titanic's* call sign MGY.

The stewards were now instructed to raise the passengers. There was no public address system so all passengers had to be alerted in person. In first and second class, this was done with a polite knock on the door and the steward advising the passengers to put on warm clothing, take a lifebelt and assemble on the deck. In third class, doors were also knocked upon, but a general call was given in the corridors to get up and put on life jackets. For the English-speaking passengers this would have been bad enough, but for those who did not understand the instructions, it must have been extremely confusing.

No need to panic

At first there was no sense of urgency. Indeed, it is likely that many of the crew did not realize just how serious the situation was. It is very unlikely that either the passengers or the crew were aware that, although there were over 2,200 people on board, there was only enough room in the lifeboats for 1178 people. In Walter Lord's book *A Night to Remember,* he mentions a conversation between a passenger, Mrs Albert Caldwell, and an unknown crew member. The lady asked, 'Is this ship really non-sinkable?' to which the crew member replied, 'Yes, lady, God himself could not sink this ship.'[2] Indeed, the mood was one of total confidence in the *Titanic*. There was no possibility that she could sink. Passengers even joked with one another that, if one were to board a lifeboat, one would need one's ticket to get back on board. However, Lawrence Beesley, a teacher travelling in second class, noticed 'an undoubted tilt downwards from stern to bow, only a slight slope.'

Nevertheless, slowly, using hand signals to communicate because of the ear-splitting din as the ship continued to let off steam, boats were uncovered, prepared and swung into position as passengers began to appear on deck. The Purser's Office was also busy, as passengers were now queuing to collect their valuables from the safe.

The action that night was split into two. It seems difficult to imagine that on one ship so many people could tell different stories but, because of the length of the superstructure, the ship was, to all intents and purposes, divided into two: the port side, where Second Officer Lightoller would take charge of the loading of lifeboats, and the starboard, where First Officer Murdoch was in control.

Slow evacuation

At 12.25 a.m., just over forty minutes after the collision, the order was given to begin to fill the lifeboats. It was also about this time that Wallace Hartley and all his musicians took up a position in the First Class Lounge where they began to play popular ragtime tunes.

In the wireless shack, Phillips and Bride were struggling to make other ships aware of their predicament. They had had several contacts but no one seemed to realize or believe the urgency of the situation. Fifty nautical miles away, Harold Thomas Cottam, wireless operator of the *Carpathia*, had been on the bridge when the original CQD had gone out. He thought it might be useful for the *Titanic* to know that she had some messages waiting. Phillips tapped back to a stunned Cottam, telling him that they had struck a berg, were sinking and asked him to come to their aid quickly. Cottam wasted no time. He raced to the cabin where his captain, Arthur Henry Rostron, was sleeping. There he advised him of the *Titanic's* plight. Five minutes later Cottam informed Phillips that they were 'coming hard'.

Note

1   **Lord, Walter,** *A Night to Remember* (London: Longmans, Green and Co.,1956) 2

2   **Lord, Walter,** *A Night to Remember* (London: Longmans, Green and Co.,1956) 38

Going down

'During all these struggles, I had been uttering silent prayers for deliverance, and it occurred to me that this was the occasion of all others, when we should join in an appeal to the Almighty as our last and only hope in life.' (Col. Archibald Gracie)[1]

This photograph was taken by a passenger on the ship that received the *Titanic's* distress signal and came to rescue the survivors. It shows the last lifeboat that had been successfully launched from the *Titanic*

Who goes first?

Although the order *Women and Children First* was given, it seems that this was interpreted in two ways. On the starboard side, Murdoch took this to mean that women and children should be loaded first, then, when they had all got on to the lifeboats, male passengers could take the remaining places. On the port side, Lightoller took it to mean that only women and children could be given places on the lifeboats. The tragedy is that in a lifeboat designed to hold sixty-five people, there were only twenty-eight passengers. It is an indication that many of the crew were unaware of the inadequate provision of lifeboats. It also shows that, when the boats were lowered in order to be filled, very few passengers were willing to enter them.

Situated in the rear of the ship on the aft docking bridge was Quartermaster George Thomas Rowe. He had seen a large iceberg passing close by and could feel that the ship was stationary, but, amazingly, he was unaware of what had taken place. It was not until lifeboat 7 passed him that he contacted the bridge to find out what was happening. A stunned Fourth Officer Boxhall instructed him to come to the bridge and to *bring rockets*.

Mystery Ship

The first rocket shot 300 feet into the air, scattering white stars as it exploded. Passengers were now beginning to suspect that something serious was happening. Both Rowe and Boxhall could see what they believed to be mast lights of another ship in the distance. In between firing rockets, they attempted to contact this 'mystery ship' with a Morse lamp. Rowe would continue firing until 1.40 a.m. and would fire eight rockets in total. The 'mystery ship' controversy still rages today.

On the bridge of the now stationary *Californian,* two of the officers noticed a strange ship in the distance and thought that she looked 'odd' in the water. At 12.45 a.m. Second Officer Herbert Stone saw the sudden flash of a white rocket. Captain Lord told them to try contacting the 'strange' ship by Morse but when this was unsuccessful, he retired to bed, telling his crew to notify him of any changes to the situation.

Back on board the *Titanic,* in the Marconi shed, Phillips was attempting to contact the *Titanic's* sister ship, *Olympic,* which was 500 miles away, sailing back to England. Bride jokingly suggested that he try the new distress call SOS and said, 'It might be the last chance you get.'[2] Down in the engine rooms, the pumps in boiler room 5 were doing a splendid job and keeping the water at bay, but the pressure behind the bulkhead was building. An order was given from the bridge that all hands were to report to boat stations. Not having had a boat drill, it is unlikely that the men knew to which boat they had to report. Suddenly, there was a deafening crash and the bulkhead dividing boiler rooms 5 and 6 gave way.

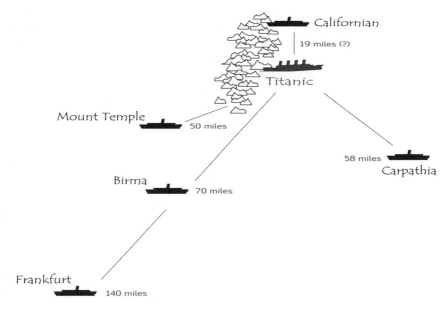

Diagram of the assumed positions of the ships in the proximity of the sinking *Titanic*

Move along now

At 12.55 a.m. lifeboat 5, on the starboard side, was launched by Fifth Officer Lowe. During the lowering, he shouted at a passenger who was telling his men to 'hurry it up'. The passenger was none other than the ship's owner, Bruce Ismay. Lowe little knew or cared; he had a job to do and he was going to do it his way. It is surprising to note that Third

Chapter 7

Officer Pitman was put in charge of the boat. Why such a high-ranking officer was required is uncertain. As the lifeboat was lowered, with just thirty-nine people on board, two male passengers jumped from the ship into the boat. Although they landed safely, they broke a couple of ribs of one of the female passengers on board. This brought the total in the boat to forty-one; there was still enough room for at least another twenty-four. At about the same time, lifeboat 6, the first lifeboat from the port side, was also being lowered under the direction of Second Officer Lightoller. On board was the notorious Margaret 'Molly' Brown, who, later in the evening, would take one of the oars and begin to row the lifeboat in order to stay warm. Under the control of Quartermaster Hichens and first-class passenger, Major Arthur Peuchen, (the only male passenger on board), lifeboat 6 was launched with just twenty-eight people on board. Again, it was woefully empty.

The action swung back and forth between starboard and port. At 1.00 a.m., with the *Titanic* settling lower in the water, lifeboat 3 was lowered on the starboard side, again under the supervision of Murdoch. Seaman George Alfred Moore was put in charge. The number reported to have been saved from this lifeboat varies between thirty-two and forty, even an optimistic fifty.

Meanwhile, on the *Californian*, the bridge crew contacted Captain Lord through a special speaking tube to advise him that the other ship was still firing rockets. Captain Lord again told them to carry on with the Morse lamp. He then rolled over and went back to sleep.

Becoming more aware of the urgency of the situation, Murdoch began to work more quickly and to launch lifeboats at a much faster pace. Moving on to what was technically called emergency boat 1, he put Lookout George Symons in charge and began to lower the boat. On board this boat were Sir Cosmo and Lady Duff Gordon and their maid, Miss Francetelli. Lady Duff Gordon and her maid were the only females on board. There were three male passengers (including Sir Duff Gordon) and seven crew members, making a total of only twelve on board a boat that was designed to hold forty.

Controversial decision

Of all the seriously under-filled boats lowered that night, this one would cause the most controversy. It is not known why Murdoch allowed the boat to leave with so few people on board. In several accounts, it is stated that Murdoch looked around for more passengers but none were standing nearby, a statement which in itself seems incredible. However, it is more likely that Murdoch thought that the *Titanic* would sink before all her lifeboats could be launched and assumed that lifeboat 1 would come back and rescue those in the water. Unfortunately for all concerned, this did not happen.

At 1.10 a.m. the action returned to the port side. Standing watching Lightoller loading boat 8, were Isidor and Ida Straus. Already on the boat, was their maid, Ellen Bird, whom they had persuaded to board. Mrs Straus, however, refused to leave her husband's side, saying, 'As we have lived, so will we die.' Colonel Archibald Gracie tried to influence the elderly Mr Straus by suggesting that he would be allowed to go too. But Isidor protested, saying, 'No, I do not wish to enter a boat before any other man.'[3] They were last seen going below, hand in hand to meet their end. Yet again the boat was lowered with only twenty-eight on board.

Moving on towards the stern, lifeboat 9, on the port side, and lifeboat 10, on the starboard side, were lowered almost simultaneously at 1.20 a.m. As the water began to reach the *Titanic's* name at the bow of the ship, a sense of urgency finally prevailed. Lifeboat 9 was lowered filled almost to capacity with fifty-six on board, mostly women. Lifeboat 10 had fifty-five people on board, men and women. As the boats were being lowered, Quartermaster Rowe fired the last of the distress rockets.

Meanwhile, in the wireless room, Phillips and Bride were frantically trying to alert all shipping to their situation. There were many ships on the Atlantic that night and most, but not all, had wireless. Tapping out the message: 'We are putting the women off in boats',4 they had several responses but most of the ships were too far away to be of any help. Even though she was 500 miles away, the Captain of the *Olympic* was determined to come to the *Titanic's* aid. The *Virginian* was 170 miles and the *Mount Temple* (like the *Carpathia*) was 50 miles away. All stated that they were on their way.

It was now approximately 1.25 a.m. First Officer Murdoch continued to load the lifeboats, but now he was beginning to take chances and he filled lifeboat 11 with seventy passengers. Rev. John Harper put his daughter, Annie, who was just six years old, and his niece, Jessie, into lifeboat 11. He stepped back, watching as they were lowered safely down to the sea. Second Officer Lightoller also continued to load women and children. Lifeboat 12 was lowered with forty-three passengers, most of them women and children from the second class.

At 1.30 a.m. Fifth Officer Lowe took charge of lifeboat 14 as it was being lowered. Filled to capacity, it had sixty passengers on board. The calm that had existed during the lowering of the other lifeboats was beginning to diminish as the water rose ever nearer the deck. The number of lifeboats still available was constantly decreasing and the desperation of the situation was becoming ever more evident. Several male passengers tried to rush the boat. Lowe fired three warning shots from the lifeboat as it was lowered.

On the starboard side, lifeboats 13 and 15 were lowered quickly one after the other—a little too quickly, perhaps, as 15 almost ended up on top of 13, the fall being cut at the very last minute, just avoiding disaster. Murdoch continued to fill the boats to capacity with sixty-four and seventy persons respectively.

We are doomed

At 1.35 a.m. Captain Smith entered the wireless cabin and told Bride and

Phillips that the engine rooms were flooded. Phillips immediately relayed the information to all shipping, again trying to urge them to come to their assistance. The last of the lifeboats at the stern on the port side was lowered with fifty-six passengers.

The action now moved back to the forward part of the ship as the crew tried to launch the Englehardt collapsibles and the last of the lifeboats. On the starboard side, Chief Officer Wilde was aided by crew members and Bruce Ismay, who had continued to help load lifeboats despite being reprimanded by Lowe. They managed somehow to load collapsible C into the davits. Quartermaster Rowe was given charge of the boat and they began lowering it with thirty-eight people on board. Almost at the last minute, Bruce Ismay stepped on board. It was a decision that would haunt him for the rest of his life and would cause him to be spurned and persecuted by many. Emergency Lifeboat 2, also on the starboard side, was lowered five minutes later with twenty-five on board. Fourth Officer Boxhall was put in charge.

Lifeboat 4, on the port side, had thirty-six passengers on board, almost all of them women. They had been waiting a long time owing to a problem with loading. Amazingly, Madeleine Astor, perhaps the richest woman on board, was only now leaving the sinking vessel. John Jacob Astor walked to the boat and passed his pregnant wife through. He politely enquired whether he might be permitted to join his wife, but stepped back to join the rest of the waiting husbands when permission was denied. Lightoller instructed those in charge on the boat to pick up more passengers from the lower aft gangway. However, the doors to the gangway were never opened. It is believed that Lightoller intended that all the boats that were launched that night should pick up more passengers from the lower aft gangway. Several swimmers would later be taken into the boat. Instead of what was once an 80 foot (24.38 m) drop to the water, was now only 15 feet (4.5 m).

Chapter 7

Times up

It was 2.05 a.m. The *Titanic* had very little time left. Captain Smith walked into the wireless shack and informed Phillips and Bride. 'It's every man for himself,'5 he said. Phillips continued to send messages in the vain hope that someone closer would come to their aid. Although Captain Smith was seen several times around the ship about this time, it is not known what happened to him in the last minutes. It is popularly thought that he went on to the bridge and went down with the ship. But we will never know for certain.

Wallace Hartley and his small band of musicians continued to play with no thought of trying to get into a lifeboat. Popular theory has them playing *Nearer My God To Thee* in the final minutes, but there are so many conflicting stories that we will never know for sure.

The electricians, who had manned their posts and kept the generators running so that the electric lifeboat davits could operate as well as all the lights, would remain there until the end, selflessly giving up their lives for others.

All the lifeboats on the port side had now been launched, but there were still more than 1500 people left on board. The situation became more aggressive and Lightoller commanded the crew to lock arms around Englehardt D. Only women and children were allowed to pass. Of the forty-seven places available on the lifeboat, only forty-four were filled.

At 2.17 a.m. the *Virginian* heard a wireless message from the *Titanic*. It read, 'CQ' and was abruptly cut short. Phillips had stayed almost until the end, but the power to the wireless generator had failed and there was little he could do. Bride and Phillips said their final farewells to each another and left the wireless shack for the last time. Bride went forward to join Lightoller and assist in his efforts to launch the last two collapsibles. Phillips went aft. This was the last time the two men would see each other.

The crew now began their struggle to launch the remaining

Englehardts. These were located on the roof of the officers' quarters, which meant that they had to be released from their moorings and then physically lifted down on to the deck. However, this proved not to be a problem as, just at that moment, the bow of the *Titanic* plunged down and a large wave knocked the struggling crew off their feet, carrying the unlaunched Englehardt B over the deck's edge where it flipped upside down. Englehardt A fared a little better and just floated off. Eleven swimmers would somehow make it theirs, but only seven would survive the night.

A dreadful predicament

As Colonel Gracie tried to head to the stern of the ship to avoid the oncoming wave, he found his way blocked by what he later described as 'a mass of humanity'.[6] He was shocked to see many women and children among them, having believed that nearly all of them had been sent off in the lifeboats. Tragically, it is now understood that many third-class passengers were kept below deck until almost the last minute. But he had little time to ponder from where they had come as he and Lightoller were washed into the sea along with many others. Dragged beneath the icy waters, they found themselves being sucked down with the ship. Only a blast of air from a vent released them, forcing them back up. Swimming towards the upturned B boat, they clambered on board and were joined by several others, among them Harold Bride. Colonel Gracie would survive the sinking but die seven months later owing to complications caused by the ordeal.

All lifeboats were gone. The gigantic stern of the *Titanic* rose out of the sea, her enormous propellers glistening in the moonlight. The lights flickered once then went out. The sounds of panic and desperation filled the air as all those left on board tried to struggle upwards towards the rear of the ship, hoping to stay out of the freezing cold water until the last minute. With the ship now at an angle of somewhere between 45 and 75 degrees, it was an almost impossible task.

As the water continued to drag the *Titanic* down, her forward funnel snapped under the strain. The mighty structure collapsed on to the starboard bridge wing before it thundered into the ocean, crushing any swimmers in the water beneath and pushing the upturned collapsible B further away from the ship.

As the mighty ship ripped herself into two, the *Titanic* let out a deafening roar as everything within her that was not bolted down emptied into the ocean. Reaching almost perpendicular, she seemed to be frozen in that one position for several moments before finally, with quickening speed, she plunged beneath the sea, dragging the poor people left on board down with her.

The time was 2.20 a.m.

Notes

1 **Gracie, Colonel Archibald,** *Titanic: A Survivor's Story* (London: Alan Sutton Publishers Ltd, 1985) 91

2 **Lord, Walter,** *A Night to Remember* (London: Longmans, Green and Co.,1956) 47

3 **Gracie, Colonel Archibald,** *Titanic: A Survivor's Story* (London: Alan Sutton Publishers Ltd, 1985) 25

4 **Lord, Walter,** *A Night to Remember* (London: Longmans, Green and Co., 1956) 64

5 **Lord, Walter,** *A Night to Remember* (London: Longmans, Green and Co., 1956) 75

6 **Gracie, Colonel Archibald,** *Titanic: A Survivor's Story* (London: Alan Sutton Publishers Ltd, 1985) 47

A terrible sound

'There is a way that seems right to a man, but in the end it leads to death,' (Proverbs 16:25).

Jack George Phillips, RMS *Titanic's* radio operator whose workload probably contributed to many deaths

O n board the *Californian*, the two officers who had watched the strange ship firing rockets noticed that she had now disappeared and they assumed that she had steamed away. They advised a sleepy Captain Lord down the speaking tube. Although it has never been established that the *Californian* was the 'mystery ship' seen by the *Titanic* or that the ship seen from the *Californian* firing rockets was the *Titanic*, or indeed just how far apart these two ships were, it is perhaps, unfortunate, that no one on the *Californian* thought to waken the wireless operator until early morning to find out what was happening.

Strange and dreadful sounds

The night air was now rent with a new sound, a terrible one. 1500 people had plunged into the freezing waters and were calling for help. These poor victims would have experienced panic, shock and disorientation. It would have taken between fifteen and forty minutes for many of them to die in the freezing water. Among them was the Rev. John Harper. In water so cold that it felt like a thousand knives penetrating skin and bone, he swam around shouting at the top of his voice, 'Are you saved?'[1]

The inevitable reply, 'no' came from many people.

John Harper's response was, 'Believe on the Lord Jesus Christ and you shall be saved.'

One man floating on top of the wreckage took up John's challenge and believed. Surviving the disaster, he would stand up some time later and declare, 'I am John Harper's last convert.' Unfortunately, his identity has never been established.

Men gathered on the upturned hull of collapsible B, which they had been unable to right. They stood all night, constantly having to readjust their weight as they were joined by others or hit by the swell of the sea. Colonel Gracie recalls that someone suggested that they recite the Lord's Prayer. All agreed.

People sitting in the lifeboats listened to the cries of the drowning. Very few made any attempt to assist them. Those who suggested that they tried were often shouted down by those who were worried about being swamped. Only Fifth Officer Lowe made any deliberate attempt to help those in the water. Rounding up boats 10, 12, 4 and D, he strung them together with his boat, 14, and rearranged the passengers. Then, with a practically empty boat, he sailed towards the drowning. Unfortunately, the transfer of passengers took time, as did the waiting for the cries to 'thin out' so that the boat would not be swamped. The physical effort needed to reach the wreck site took even longer. By the time boat 14 reached the people, nearly an hour had passed. Only four people were pulled to safety from the sea and one of them died within the hour.

Quiet descends over the whole scene

Gradually, the cries of the drowning got fewer and fewer, and then ceased altogether. A state of quiet shock now descended on the approximately 700 in the lifeboats—this figure is still not certain. Shooting stars lit up the night sky. Indeed, many survivors reported an unusual amount of stellar activity that night. Suddenly, the reverie was broken as a green flare was lit. It was Fourth Officer Boxhall in boat 2, who was trying to attract the attention of any ships in the area. They were not out of danger yet. Small lifeboats adrift in the ocean could still be lost!

On the upturned collapsible B, thoughts also turned to being rescued. Lightoller had taken control, arranging the thirty men into two rows so as to balance the weight on the boat. He would call out, 'Lean left' or 'Lean right'[2] whenever necessary to counteract the swell of the sea. Bride was also on board and he advised his fellow passengers that the *Olympic*, the *Baltic* and the *Carpathia* were on their way.

The *Carpathia* was indeed on her way. Primarily a Hungarian immigrant ship, the *Carpathia* had been launched by Cunard in 1903. Her top speed was only 14.5 knots, but, amazingly, she achieved a record 17.5 knots that night.

It seemed like a very long time since Marconi operator, Harold Cottam, had burst into the Captain's stateroom with news that the *Titanic* was sinking. Captain Arthur Henry Rostron had not wasted any time. Requesting an immediate change of course (they had been going to sail the Mediterranean), he began to give orders while getting dressed. All lifeboats were to be swung out for the rescue. Their English doctor would attend to all first-class passengers, the Italian doctor would care for the second class and the Hungarian doctor would look after the third class. Hot soup, tea, and coffee were to be prepared and as many blankets as could be found were to be collected. Stewards were to be posted in all corridors to keep the *Carpathia's* passengers out of the way. Heating and hot water were to be turned off in order to generate as much steam as possible.

Harold Cottam had returned to his wireless shack and was now aided by a steward who would act as a runner and relay all messages. All telegrams were sent directly to the bridge; the news was not good.

The *Carpathia's* passengers were beginning to notice that something was amiss. It was getting colder; there was no heating in the cabins. When the passengers rang for a steward or looked out of their doors to see what was happening, they were politely, but firmly, asked to stay in their cabins.

In Walter Lord's second book about the tragedy *The Night Lives On*, he described Captain Rostron as 'a very pious man, who never smoked, drank or used profanity and would frequently turn to prayer. When he did so, he would lift his uniform cap slightly and his lips would move in silent supplication.'[3] Knowing that he had to face the same problems with the ice that had sunk the *Titanic*, and knowing that he was responsible for the 700 lives on board the *Carpathia*, and also knowing that time was of the essence, Captain Rostron did just that, and was seen by fellow crew members lifting his cap.

At 3.00 a.m. a green flare was spotted on the horizon; it was Boxhall's. At 3.30 a.m. Rostron gave the order to fire the rockets, one every fifteen minutes, to let the survivors know that help was on its way. By 4.00 a.m. the *Carpathia* reached the *Titanic's* last known position but there was nothing to be seen, just a huge ice field. Captain Rostron would later state: 'When day broke, and I saw the ice I had steamed through during the night, I shuddered, and could only think that some Hand other than mine was on the helm during the night.'[4]

There they are

As dawn broke, the *Titanic's* lifeboats could be seen. Rostron manoeuvred his ship into a better position to pick up survivors. At 4.10

Group of survivors on board the *Carpathia* after being rescued

a.m. the women from boat 2 began to climb aboard; they were the first to be rescued. Slowly the rest of the lifeboats began to arrive, their passengers were quickly processed by the able crew of the *Carpathia*. As each boat arrived, an awful realization hit the survivors—many of their friends and loved ones had not survived. Many of the women survivors believed that their husbands would be on another boat and would join them later. The dreadful truth was now beginning to dawn. Indeed, of the 2,228 crew and passengers on board the *Titanic*, only a woeful 705 had survived. Numbers have varied over the years from 701 to 713 because of inadequate records.

The *Carpathia's* passengers were beginning to realize that something was going on. What started as a rumour among them now became cold, harsh reality. Rising to the situation that had been thrust upon them, many of them offered clothing and comfort to the survivors, irrespective of which class they had travelled.

On collapsible B, Lightoller was having great difficulty keeping his craft afloat as the swell of the sea picked up and threatened to overwhelm the upturned vessel. Afraid that they would get overlooked and left behind, he began to blow on his whistle. Finally, lifeboat 12 came alongside and took them on board. The poor men who had stood all night were eventually rescued. Lightoller was the last to leave the boat and the last survivor to board the *Carpathia*.

With all safely on board, Captain Rostron gave the order for one final sweep of the wreck site to be made. They were now joined by the *Californian*, whose officers, upon seeing the *Carpathia's* rockets, finally woke up their wireless operator who received the horrific news. However, there was very little they could do at this stage and many of the ships that had responded to the *Titanic's* distress call now resumed their original course. Leaving the *Californian* to continue the search for survivors, Rostron set sail for New York, taking those on board his ship with him.

There was one more sad duty for the *Carpathia* to perform. A third-class, male passenger had been taken on board dead from Collapsible A and three male crew survivors, who had reached the relative safety of the *Carpathia*, had been overcome by shock and exposure. They died shortly after boarding. They would all be buried at sea.

Tell us what happened

By now a news-hungry world was waiting to hear the fate of the *Titanic*. Having picked up garbled Marconi messages, the media knew that something had happened. But many newspapers had headlines which confidently stated: '*Titanic* strikes iceberg—All Saved' or that the *Titanic* is 'Being Towed', again unable to believe that the mighty ship could have foundered. Rumours abounded as family members of crew and passengers began to gather at the White Star Line's offices, desperate for news. But it was not until Tuesday, 16 April that the dreadful fate of the ship and its passengers was confirmed.

Having been on duty for more than twenty-four hours sending and receiving messages, young Harold Cottam's job was far from over. To him now fell the task of advising the world of the names of the survivors. Understandably, he was overwhelmed. Even though his feet were in bandages because of frostbite, Harold Bride agreed after a brief rest to help Cottam. Between the two of them, names began to be relayed to the *Olympic* which would then transfer the information to Cape Race.

As the names were posted at the White Star Line's offices, there were occasional shouts of joy, but, on the whole, there were cries of despair as the search for a loved one's name brought no happy results. The figures read like this:

		Survived	Perished
First-Class Passengers:	Male	57	118
	Female	140	4
	Children	5	1
Second-Class Passengers:	Male	14	154
	Female	80	13
	Children	24	0
Third-Class Passengers:	Male	75	387
	Female	76	89
	Children	27	52
Crew:	Male	192	693
	Female	20	3

(All figures vary according to different sources)[5]

Plagued by constant requests from the newspapers for information, Captain Rostron imposed a news blackout. Only the names of survivors were to be broadcast. Approaching New York on 18 April, the *Carpathia* was flanked by a flotilla of little boats, many of which had been hired by reporters to approach the ship. Some reporters bribed their way on to the pilot vessel, but were repelled by the crew of the *Carpathia*. Only one reporter made it on to the ship itself and he was taken to Captain Rostron who commanded him to stay on the bridge.

We are all in this together!

As the *Carpathia* approached the harbour, a storm blew up, thunder and lightning ripped across the sky and strong winds buffeted the ship. Crowds of more than 10,000 gathered to see the spectacle, watching almost in silence the scenes unfold in the flashes of lightning. Making her way to the White Star Line's piers 59 and 60, the *Carpathia* unloaded the *Titanic's* lifeboats which she had taken on board, and then, slowly, she headed for the Cunard pier, pier 54. By 9.30 p.m. she was finally moored and the gangways lowered. Relatives and reporters pressed forward as the first of the survivors descended.

The scene was almost surreal with the flashes of cameras adding to the flashes of lightning that lit up the night. Confused and exhausted, first and second-class survivors were either embraced by love ones or taken off to hospital in waiting ambulances. Mrs Charles Hays, widow of the President of the Grand Trunk Railroad, was whisked away in a private train.

There was no such welcome committee for the third-class passengers. Many of them had left families behind or lost them in the sinking. They had also lost all their possessions and paperwork and although they were spared the rigours of Ellis Island, immigration officials had boarded the *Carpathia* to start the procedure. Finally, at 11.00 p.m., when they began to emerge, much of the crowd and all of the reporters had dispersed. Very few were interested in these poor wretched souls. Many of them, predominately women, would have to rely on the charity of the American Red Cross or the Women's Relief Committee for support.

Finally, last to leave the *Carpathia* was the *Titanic's* crew. Many of them had lost their identification papers as well as their wages which would have ceased as the *Titanic* sank beneath the waves. They were ushered off quietly, out of public view, so that they would not have to face questioning. Taken to the moored Red Star Line's *Lapland*, they were given third-class berths; the four surviving officers were housed in the first class. However, they would all find themselves held 'captive' in New York for questioning

Rescued lifeboats: all that is left from the great ship, *Titanic*, New York, 1912

at the American Inquiry that would follow. With her duty done, the *Carpathia* silently slipped away from pier 54 and headed back out to sea, taking her original passengers back to the Mediterranean.

Notes

1 **Adams, Moody,** *Titanic's Last Hero* (Belfast, Northern Ireland: Ambassador Productions Ltd, 1998) 20

2 **Lord, Walter,** *A Night to Remember* (London: Longmans, Green and Co., 1956) 114

3 **Lord, Walter,** *The Night Lives On* (Middlesex, England: Viking, 1987) 155

4 **Lord, Walter,** *A Night to Remember* (London: Longmans, Green and Co.,1956) 129

5 **Lord, Walter,** *A Night to Remember* (London: Longmans, Green and Co.,1956) 154; **Lord, Walter,** *The Night Lives On* (Middlesex, England: Viking, 1987) 92 and web site: www.anesi.com/titanic.htm (Casualty Figures)

Coming to Halifax

'The seas have lifted up their voice,' (Psalm 93:3).

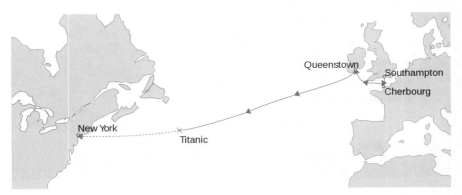

Map marks the route of the *Titanic* during her maiden voyage, the ports on that route, and approximate location where she sank. The remaining portion of her uncompleted route is shown by the dotted line

A sombre task

At around 12.30 p.m. on Wednesday 17 April, while the *Carpathia* was still on her journey to New York, another ship set sail. The CS *Mackay-Bennett*, a cable laying ship, quietly slipped her moorings in Halifax, Nova Scotia and headed out to sea. Chartered by White Star Line, the crew, all volunteers, led by Captain F. H. Lardner, had the unenviable task of recovering the dead.

On board was a cargo of coffins, ice, embalming fluid and canvas bags—everything that was needed to perform the sad and terrible duty. Also on board was Canon Kenneth Cameron Hind of All Saints Cathedral (Halifax) and John R. Snow Jnr, chief embalmer of the company of undertakers, Snow & Company.

Travelling over 700 miles, it was a difficult journey owing to bad weather. Fog and rough seas slowed them down and it was not until late on Saturday, 20 April that they finally arrived at the site of the wreck. Most other shipping was avoiding the area for obvious reasons: the sea was littered with debris and bodies.

Retrieval

It seems strange that with the sheer number of missing persons, the *Mackay-Bennett* had only 100 coffins on board. The news blackout imposed by Captain Rostron and the general incredulity that the mighty *Titanic* could have sunk, were, possibly, the reasons for these inadequate preparations. Perhaps they did not think that there would be that many victims. When they arrived at the site, the crew must have been daunted and appalled by the task before them. However, they set to work in the early hours of Sunday morning, lowering the small rowing boat. Even though they had to battle heavy seas, they managed to recover fifty-one bodies.

As each body was taken on board, it was given a number, which was stencilled on to a canvas sheet. A description of the person was written down, including any distinguishing marks such as scars or birthmarks. Any possessions found on the body were put into a small canvas bag bearing the person's number. Occasionally, they were able to identify the victim by papers found on the body. In these cases, they would contact Halifax by wireless with the name. Most of the victims had to be identified later. The bodies were then wrapped in the canvas sheet and placed either in a pine coffin or buried at sea.

The decision to bury some of the victims at sea later caused upset and controversy at home. Was this done because some were beyond recognition or, as has been suggested, because they were third-class passengers? This is another one of those mysteries to which we will never know the answer.

Chapter 9

In his book *End of a dream,* Wyn Craig Wade quotes from a diary kept by Frederick Hamilton, an engineer on board the *Mackay-Bennett*:

'The tolling of the bell summoned all hands to the forecastle where thirty bodies are to be committed to the deep, each carefully weighted and carefully sewed up in canvas. It is a weird scene, this gathering. The crescent moon is shedding a faint light on us, as the ship lays wallowing in the great rollers. The funeral service is conducted by the Reverend Canon Hind; for nearly an hour the words: "For as much as it hath pleased … we therefore commit his body to the deep" are repeated and at each interval comes, splash! As the weighted body plunges into the sea, there to sink to a depth of about two miles. Splash, splash, splash.'[1]

An unknown child

Captain Lardner began to realize the enormity of the task set before them and asked for help. On Thursday, 25 April the CS *Minia* set sail for the wreck site. As the *Mackay-Bennett* turned for home, leaving the *Minia* to carry on the work, she had 190 bodies on board. The crew had buried 116 at sea. Of those on board, one was the body of John Jacob Astor IV, the richest man on the *Titanic* and, by contrast, there was also the body of a small, fair-haired child of approximately two years, believed to be from the third class. Death knows no distinction.

The *Minia* would recover only seventeen more bodies, two of which would be buried at sea. It was joined by the SS *Montmagny* who would recover a further three. A total of 337 were recovered, most of them by the aforementioned ships and some by passing vessels. But the question on the minds of many would be: 'Where were the rest of the victims?' Owing to the bad weather and the proximity of the Gulf Stream, it is likely that they were just swept away.

On 30 April 1912 the *Mackay-Bennett* docked in Halifax and in the privacy of the walled quay unloaded her precious cargo. The coffins were placed on horse-drawn hearses and transported to the Mayflower Curling

Rink, which was set up as a temporary morgue. It was divided into cubicles by canvas sheets in order to offer privacy to visiting relatives. Everything was done to protect the dignity of the dead from mawkish sightseers so identification was asked of every relative who came to try and find a loved one. John Jacob Astor was the first to be reclaimed.

Reclaimed

Burials began in May in Fairview Lawn Cemetery. Those that were identified have names carved on to the granite blocks above where they lie; those unidentified have just a number on the block—the number they were given by the *Mackay-Bennett*. On 4 May there was a special burial: the little, fair-haired boy of about two years of age had remained unidentified and unclaimed. Touched by his plight, the crew took on the responsibility and paid for his funeral themselves, erecting a special headstone which was inscribed 'to an unknown child'. With the advancement of DNA research, many attempts have been made to identify the body of the boy. In April 2011, after several failed attempts, he was positively identified as Sidney Leslie Goodwin, youngest son of Fred and Augusta Goodwin. He was just nineteen months old. His parents were travelling with their six children in third class. They all perished in the tragedy.

A whitewash

The survivors, the relatives and the general public were hungry for answers. There would be two inquiries into the disaster. The American one, held by Senator William Alden Smith, would conclude that Captain Smith and his crew were more than partly to blame for the sinking and the inadequate filling of the lifeboats; that the British Board of Trade and White Star Line were to blame for allowing a ship of that size to sail with so few lifeboats; and that Captain Lord of the *Californian* should not have failed to respond to a cry of distress.

Account written by hand on 15 April 1912 by the Captain of RMS *Carpathia*, describing his response to the distress signal of the *Titanic*

In the British Inquiry, Lord John Charles Bigham Mersey would conclude that Captain Smith and his crew were not to blame; that the provision of lifeboats, although inadequate, was in keeping with the current Board of Trade regulations; and that Captain Lord should have responded to the rockets. The American Inquiry would be labelled 'a farce' and the British one 'a whitewash'.

Many of the survivors would suffer from mental and, in some cases, physical scars for the rest of their lives. In Judith B. Geller's book *Titanic: Women and Children First*, she writes: 'The more resilient gave thanks for their survival by helping others. For those who could not recover, it was a big enough job just to get through each day. Through all their lives runs the common thread of a reluctance to discuss 15 April 1912, but the darker consequences of alcoholism, multiple marriages and depression also occur.'[2]

Into Legend

It is not surprising, perhaps, with so many unanswered questions, that folklore and myths soon sprung up concerning the *Titanic*. One rumour has it that during construction a riveter was walled up inside her. Those working on the ship could hear his ghostly tappings as he tried to find his way out. It may sound ridiculous, but this is what people began to say! There is no evidence that such a thing happened and the ghostly tappings were probably just the rivets cooling down.

Another has it that the number given the *Titanic* by Harland & Wolff spelt *no pope* if held up to a mirror. In a country where many Roman Catholics lived, this caused an outrage, and led to the belief that the *Titanic* was cursed from the start. Again, there is no truth in this. The number given to the *Titanic* by Harland & Wolff was 401. Even if you take the number 131,428, given to her by the Board of Trade, it will not spell anything when held up to a mirror!

3909 04

ИО РОРЕ

The erroneous *no pope* number of the *Titanic*

There was also the belief that the owners had claimed that the *Titanic* was 'unsinkable'. This, too, was just the result of rumours circulated by the press after the event.

Another was the story of the 'Mummy's Curse'. Legend has it that the mummy and sarcophagus of Princess Amen-Ra were loaded into the cargo hold of the *Titanic*. From that moment the *Titanic* was cursed, as the mummy wreaked vengeance from beyond the grave. It was even said that the owner somehow managed to get the mummy case into a lifeboat and bribed the crew of the *Carpathia* to take it on board—quite an achievement in itself! Later it was supposedly put on board the RMS *Empress of Ireland* for transport back to England but on 29 May 1914, the *Empress of Ireland* collided with a coal ship and sank in just fourteen minutes with great loss of life. That is another story! Another version has it being loaded on board the RMS *Lusitania* which sank on 7 May 1915, after being torpedoed by a German submarine. Had the curse struck again? Of course, the story is completely fabricated. The mummy case is not of Princess Amen-Ra, but an unnamed Theban priestess from the twenty-first dynasty. It is incorrectly known as the 'unlucky mummy' and can be seen in the British Museum. It has never left the Museum premises since it was placed in the Egyptian collection in 1889. For any who wish to see it, the museum's number for it is EA 22542. If it is on display, the helpful staff will point it out.

Sisters

Britannic, formerly *Gigantic*, would go on to see active duty during World War I. Being renamed HMHS *Britannic*, she was used as a hospital ship. Unfortunately, on 21 November 1916, she struck a mine off the Greek island of Kea and sank in fifty-five minutes, a lot quicker than the *Titanic* did. This time thirty lives were lost. The myths and legends were once again revived!

Of *Titanic's* two sister ships, only the *Olympic* would survive to a decent age. Serving in World War I as a troop ship, she earned the nickname 'old reliable' which, considering the fate of her siblings, is quite remarkable. At the grand old age of twenty-four, she was retired and sold for scrap, finally being decommissioned in 1937.

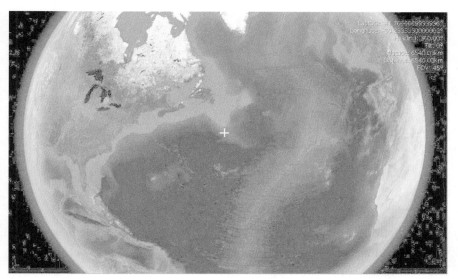

Photograph taken from space, showing the approximate location of the wreck of the *Titanic*. The white cross marks the reported position of the *Titanic* (41°46'N 50°14'W)

Notes

1 **Wade, Wyn Craig,** *The Titanic: End of a Dream* (London: George Weidenfeld and Nicolson Ltd, 1986) 67

2 **Geller, Judith B.,** *Titanic: Women and Children First* (Yeovil, Somerset, England: Patrick Stephens Ltd, 1998) 11

Chapter 10

Where are you?

'I cannot imagine any condition which would cause a ship to founder. I cannot conceive of any vital disaster happening to this vessel. Modern shipbuilding has gone beyond that.'

Captain Smith, upon assuming the captaincy of the *Adriatic*[1]

The *Titanic* was gone, but certainly not forgotten. Thoughts and plans turned to her recovery by raising her from the ocean bed, but two world wars and a lack of funds would prevent this from happening too soon.

There she is!

With the introduction of underwater exploration, the *Titanic* once again became the prize. This mighty ship, however, eluded all attempts at being located until 1 September 1985 when, under a French/American flag, her final resting place was discovered.

The expedition was split into two phases. The first was headed up by the French. Leading that team was Jean-Louis Michel who arrived on site on 5 July 1985. He began with a sonar search of the area where the *Titanic's* last reported position was thought to be. They were later joined by the American team leader, Robert (Bob) Ballard. Together they searched for many weeks, often hindered by terrible weather. Nothing was found.

On 12 August, the American team took over the search. Jean-Louis Michel joined them. Bob Ballard suggested that they change tactics and, instead of looking for the ship herself, look for the *Titanic's* debris field. In addition to a sonar search, they would use 'state of the art' underwater

Front cover of *The New York Herald*, 15 April 1912, with the first public details of the ship's sinking

cameras. By working in shifts, they would be able to search twenty-four hours a day. They would also widen the search area, using the *Californian's* logbook to calculate just how far the *Titanic* may have drifted.

However, in spite of their best efforts, the *Titanic* was not found until the last few days of the expedition. It was during the early hours of 1 September that the first 'shaky' images of one of the *Titanic's* boilers came into view. The expedition would follow the debris trail for nearly 600 yards before it reached the prow of the *Titanic* herself. In the four and a half days that remained, the team would take hundreds of photographs. Real exploration of the wreck would not take place until the team returned the following year.

A sad sight

Two and a half miles down on the ocean floor, the once-beautiful liner was now in two pieces. Her bow section stood upright, but all four of her smokestacks (funnels) and her rigging were gone. The grand, elegant staircase was missing. All that was left where it had once stood was a gaping hole. All of her wooden decking had disappeared, either ripped away by the sheer pressure of the water as she sank or eaten by micro-organisms. Parts of the superstructure were still evident but her bridge was missing. Even the metal hull was slowly being corroded, decaying into what Bob Ballard would nickname 'rusticles'. In spite of this tragic sight, the *Titanic's* bow was still impressive. Her stern was not so. Separated by nearly 2,000 feet from the bow position, was the *Titanic's* stern. Although upright, it was not a pleasant sight. Many of the decks had collapsed on top of one another in a twisted wreck of metal, surrounded by debris. Just like her bow, the stern was buried up to forty feet in the mud at the bottom of the ocean. Scientists who have studied the bacteria that is destroying the *Titanic* estimate that, within thirty to fifty years, she will collapse and within the next hundred years she will disappear altogether.

Leaving just a memorial plaque and taking nothing from the site, Bob Ballard and his team ended their search, hoping that the *Titanic* would be left alone as a monument to those who died on her tragic maiden voyage. Unfortunately, this was not to be the case.

There have been many legal wrangles over who owns the site, as the *Titanic* could now be termed as 'salvage'. Many expeditions have taken place to recover artefacts which are now on display in special exhibitions all over the world. In August 1996 an expedition led by the French attempted to raise a section of the ship's hull. Weighing in at 20 tons and measuring 25 by 15 feet, it would be affectionately nicknamed 'the big piece'. With a huge media presence, and watched by passengers on two cruise liners who had paid staggering amounts to secure a ticket, the large section was inched towards the surface. However, with just 200 feet to go, the raising mechanism gave way and 'the big piece' once again sank beneath the waves. Two years later another attempt would be successful.

An obsession

In 1997 film director, James Cameron, released his movie *Titanic* which tells of a highly improbable love story between a first and third-class passenger. He found himself obsessed with the subject. By spending millions of his own money, he visited the site of the wreck several times and filmed it extensively. He has probably visited it more times than anyone else! In 2003 Cameron released a 3D movie *Ghosts of the Abyss*, a documentary allowing viewers to see the *Titanic* for themselves and even view inside the wreck.

All the expeditions, films and media coverage of the *Titanic* have only increased the public's fascination for her. Perhaps it is because she is still elusive, an enigma, or perhaps—in spite of all that we know about her—there is still so much that is unanswered and will probably remain so.

A sad reminder

Rev. Stuart Holden of St Paul's, Portman Square, London was an evangelical clergyman and a leading Keswick Convention preacher, who was due to sail on the *Titanic*. He cancelled his trip because his wife was ill. Instead of perishing in 1912, he lived and preached for another twenty-two years. He framed his ticket and put it above his desk in his study, where it remained for the rest of his life, as a reminder of his being redeemed for a purpose. Underneath it, he wrote a line from Psalm 103: '... who redeemeth thy life from destruction'. This served as a daily reminder to him. His escape from the disaster had a profound effect upon the way he viewed his life and ministry.

Note

1 **Lord, Walter,** *A Night to Remember* (London: Longmans, Green and Co.,1956) 24

What if?

'The Moving Finger writes; and, having writ, moves on.'

Rubaiyat of Omar Khayyamm, Poem 545,
a priceless copy of which was on board the *Titanic*[1]

Edward J. Smith, captain of the *Titanic*, who went down with his ship. This photograph was taken on board the *Olympic* by an unknown photographer and was published following the sinking in 1912

There were many random factors involved in the events of the night of 15 April 1912. Indeed, it has been called one of the biggest 'ifs' in history. 'What if' just one of these factors had been changed? What then might have been the outcome? Here are a few possibilities we could consider.

What if the *Titanic's* maiden voyage had been delayed?

In February 1912 nearly all the coal mines in the United Kingdom were closed down owing to a coal miners' strike. Many shipping lines found their businesses severely affected. Although by 6 April the strike was finally over, there was no time to transport newly-mined coal to the *Titanic*. In order that her maiden voyage would not be delayed, White Star Line had to beg and borrow coal from its other liners. Many passengers, who had booked to sail on other liners, found themselves transferred to the *Titanic*. Some not only suffered the inconvenience of having their sailing dates changed but also of being downgraded on their cabin assignment. If White Star Line had been unable to 'borrow' the necessary 7,000 tons of coal required, it is unlikely that the *Titanic* would have been ready to set sail on 10 April 1912. Had that been the case, the 'ice field' into which she sailed would probably have moved by the time she made her voyage.

It is also worth taking into consideration the fire in the coalbunker. If this had been more serious, it would have caused a delay in the departure date.

What if the *Titanic* had collided with the SS *New York*?

There is no doubt that if this had happened, White Star Line would have had no choice but to delay the maiden voyage and assess the damage caused by the collision. The narrow shave the *Titanic* experienced when departing from Southampton was seen by many as 'quick thinking on the part of Captain Smith'. Others saw it as ominous.

What if the *Titanic* had taken a more southerly route?

Icebergs were not a new hazard to shipping. They had been a problem since the beginning of transatlantic travel. The *Titanic* was not the first liner to hit an iceberg. In 1879 the SS *Arizona* had collided with a berg. She was certainly not the last. However, in order to avoid this dangerous hazard, there were two recognized routes taken by shipping across the

Atlantic. The quicker Northern route was usually travelled during the summer months and the more southerly route taken in the winter. There has been much debate as to the route that the *Titanic* was actually taking. It is generally believed, however, to have been the more southerly route. It was noted at the two inquiries that icebergs had travelled further south than had ever been seen before. At the British Inquiry, Bruce Ismay stated that because of the sinking of the *Titanic*, the 'southerly' route was moved 150 miles further south. Also, as a direct result of the disaster, the International Ice Patrol would be set up and an even more southerly route would be enforced.

What if the *Titanic* had slowed down?
Captain Smith was following the common practice of the day when he kept up speed. Many sea captains called to the British Inquiry agreed that they would have done the same. However, if Captain Smith had been aware of all of the iceberg warnings and if they had been plotted on the chart in the map room, then, perhaps, he would have slowed down. The Inquiry did not condemn Captain Smith for his actions but it did state that, in future, any captain facing similar circumstances would be charged with negligence if he did not reduce speed.

What if the *Titanic* had hit the iceberg head on?
There has been a lot of research carried out in the years since the *Titanic* went down. Generally, the view is held that if she had hit the iceberg head on instead of scraping along her starboard side, the *Titanic* would not have sunk. There would have been considerable damage and people in the forward section would probably have been killed or hurt, but she would still have been able to limp on to New York.

What if the *Titanic* had had enough lifeboats?
One can only surmise what may have happened if the original plans of

Alexander Carlisle (a Managing Director of Harland & Wolff) had been followed and sixty-four lifeboats had been fitted on the *Titanic*. There would have been enough room for everyone. But would there have been enough time to load them all? As it was, they were still trying to load boats as the ship began to sink below the water.

There was a forty-minute time lapse between hitting the iceberg and the lowering of the first lifeboat. If a 'lifeboat drill' had been carried out on the Sunday morning, as it should have been, possibly things would have moved a little faster.

With only sixteen lifeboats and four small collapsible boats for the approximately 2,228 passengers and crew, the *Titanic* did not have an adequate number of lifesaving vessels. After the *Titanic* sank, the public demanded stricter rules regarding lifeboats. The Seaman's Act of 1915 stipulated that the number of passengers on a ship, not the gross tonnage, would determine the number of lifeboats necessary.

What if the *Titanic* had fully loaded all its lifeboats?

The capacity of the lifeboats she had is listed at 1178. Simple mathematics shows us that a further 350 lives could have been saved if they had been filled to capacity and, perhaps, a few more if they had been 'over filled'. Concerns about capsizing during the lowering of the boats were raised as one of the reasons why this was not done. Also, they had the intention of picking up passengers from another part of the ship. However, when we consider that the *Titanic* was designed to hold 3,328 passengers and crew, had she been filled to capacity, the death toll could have been much higher.

In the Bible, there is the record of a great flood that covered the whole earth. We are told that this happened at a time of great wickedness on the earth—people sinned against one another and against God. Before it came, God instructed a man called Noah to build a big ship called an Ark and to warn people that the earth was going to be flooded. However, they refused to listen to Noah's message, thinking it absurd that such a thing could ever take place. The time finally came for God to shut Noah, his family and the animals that had gathered into the Ark. God then flooded the earth with water and, in this way, judged all people for their sin against him. During the great flood, only a few people were saved, even though God had previously shown great patience towards the people of Noah's generation (1 Peter 3:20). Today, the Bible speaks of the gift of salvation for all who trust in the Lord Jesus Christ, the only Saviour (Acts 4:12). How sad it is that Noah pleaded in vain for people to respond to his message and, finally, it was God who shut the door of the Ark with only Noah, his family and the animals safely inside. All others were shut out (Genesis 7:16). Although that was an event that took place a very long time ago, its lesson still speaks to us today. God clearly speaks to us in a number of ways: through creation (Romans 1:20); by our consciences (Romans 2:14–16); through his Son, the Lord Jesus Christ (Hebrews 1:2); and in his Word, the Bible (2 Timothy 3:16–17). The Lord Jesus uses the history of Noah and the Ark to warn people about his second coming, to instruct them about what will happen to them if they have not repented of their sin and cried out to him to save them (Matthew 24:37–39). How tragic it will be if we continue to live our lives as though they will last for ever on earth!

What if the 'mystery ship' had responded?

We will never know for certain the name of the ship that the *Titanic* could see so tantalizingly near. There have been many suggestions as to the identity of the ship: the *Californian*, the *Mount Temple*, the *Samson*. None has been proven beyond doubt to be the 'mystery ship'. Indeed, it has even been suggested that in those strange weather conditions that night, there was no ship at all and that the lights that were seen were just an odd reflection of the *Titanic's* own lights. However, if there was a ship there and if it had responded to the distress call, or if the *Californian* had

had twenty-four hour Marconi operation and had responded to the *Titanic's* distress call, then the loss of life would probably have been minimal.

What if?

Twelve thousand men spent almost two years in Belfast on the construction of the *Titanic*. It is sobering to think that a glancing blow from an iceberg caused the massive vessel to sink and not be traced for as many as seventy-three years. The largest and most luxurious ship the world had ever known was helpless against the forces of nature. So many died because of the arrogant overestimation of man's power.

The first assertion of the *Titanic's* unsinkable nature appeared in the *New York Times* on Tuesday, 16 April 1912. A quote from Philip A. S. Franklin, vice President of the White Star Line, reportedly stated: 'I thought her unsinkable and I based my opinion on the best expert advice available. I do not understand it.'[2]

As stated earlier, the second-class passenger, Mrs Albert Caldwell— she and her husband were missionaries in Bangkok, Thailand, as teachers in a Christian College for boys—later remembered that she had asked one of the deckhands at Southampton whether the *Titanic* was truly unsinkable. He supposedly responded, 'Yes, Lady, God himself could not sink this ship.' Even if this thought is not expressed exactly as she remembered it, the sentiment well sums up the folly of man in the face of God.

We can ask the question 'what if' many times through history. What if more people had decided to read the Bible, go to church, heed the lessons of a godly member of their family? There are so many wasted opportunities as individuals hurtle headlong through life, without taking time to stop and think about the truly big questions of life. What if there really is a God? What if I have to give an account of my life on a day of Judgement? What if Jesus Christ really did die to save me from my sins?

Listen to Calvin

In a brilliant passage on the brevity of life and on the many dangers found in this life, John Calvin wrote in his *Institutes of the Christian Religion* (1559) the following:

'Innumerable are the ills which beset human life, and present death in as many different forms. Not to go beyond ourselves, since the body is a receptacle of a thousand diseases, a man cannot move along without carrying along with him many forms of destruction. His life is interwoven with death. For what else can be said where heat and cold bring equal danger? Then, in whatever direction you turn, all surrounding objects not

John Calvin, the French reformer, whose powerful words regarding the constant danger we face are still as powerful as when they were first spoken

only may do harm, but almost openly threaten and seem to present immediate death. Go on board a ship, you are a plank's breath away from death. Mount a horse, the stumbling of your foot endangers your life. Walk along the streets, every tile upon the roofs is a source of danger. If a sharp instrument is in your hand, or that of a friend, the possible harm is manifest. All the savage beasts you see are so many beings armed for your destruction. Even within a high-walled garden, where everything ministers to delight, a serpent will sometimes lurk. Your house, constantly exposed to fire, threatens you with poverty by day, with destruction at night. Your fields, subject to hail, mildew, drought, and other injuries, denounce barrenness, and thereby famine. I say nothing of poison, treachery, robbery, some of which beset us at home, others follow us abroad. Amid these perils, must not man be very miserable, as one who, more dead than alive, with difficulty draws an anxious and feeble breath, just as if a drawn sword were constantly suspended over his neck?

It may be said that these things happen seldom, at least not always, or to all, certainly never at once. I admit it; but since we are reminded by the example of others, that they may happen to us, and that our life is not an exception any more than theirs, is it impossible not to fear and dread as if they were to befall us?'[3]

False hope

If only people would stop and consider their lives today, what could be the result? Too many have a false hope not based on fact. On the front page of the *London Times* for Tuesday, 16 April 1912, was the following announcement:

The *Titanic* Sunk

The following message was received as we were going to press:—
New York, April 15th
The *Titanic* sank at 2.20 this morning. No lives were lost. (Reuter)[4]

How many think that their lives are good enough for God to accept them and that they will end up in his heaven after death!

After the sinking of the *Titanic*, relatives and friends of the passengers gathered outside the White Star Line's offices in Liverpool, England. As news filtered through, the passengers' names were placed on one of two lists: 'Known to be saved' or 'Known to be lost'. A voyage that had begun with passengers of all ranks, status and position ended with them reduced to only two, saved or lost.

The mighty ship *Titanic* was lost and, though the wreck has now been found, it is in a sorry state compared to its former glory. The Lord Jesus said that when people put their trust in him, they go from the first list to the second, from lost to found. The Bible tells us that God has set a standard by which we are to live. But all have refused to accept that standard and have chosen to go their own way. The Bible calls this sin, which is breaking God's law (1 John 3:4). All sin is wrongdoing (1 John 5:17), which means that everyone is guilty. God holds us accountable for our refusal to obey his laws and, at our death, he will judge us and punish us for our disobedience. The truly good news is that we do not have to despair. In love, God sent his Son, the Lord Jesus Christ, to bear the wrath of God against sinners and to take our punishment by dying on the cross. All those who turn to the Lord Jesus Christ in repentance and faith will have their sins forgiven them and will be saved by him from God's wrath. In heaven, they will appear far more glorious than at any time during their earthly existence.

In 1902, after an operation for appendicitis, King Edward VII shook hands with Joseph Lister, the famous surgeon, and said, 'Lord Lister, I know well that if it had not been for you and your work, I should not be here today.'[5] On the great day of judgement that is coming, there will be many who will point back to the cross of Jesus Christ and say, 'If it were not for you, Jesus, I would not be saved for ever!'

Notes

1 *The Rubaiyat of Omar Khayyam,* Poem 545, translated by Edward J. Fitzgerald, found at www.wonderingminstrels.blogspot.com/2000/09/moving-finger-writes-a.

2 Quoted in the *New York Times,* taken from a Souvenir Facsimile edition of the front cover of *The Times* of London, 1912 (Copyright: *The Times,* 1998)

3 **Calvin, John,** *Institutes of the Christian Religion,* Vol. 1, translated by **Henry Beveridge** (Grand Rapids, MI: Wm. B. Eerdmans Publishing Co., Eighth Printing, 1979) Book First: Of the knowledge of God the creator, 192–193

4 Quotation from *The Times,* taken from a Souvenir Facsimile edition of the front cover of *The Times* of London, 1912 (Copyright: *The Times,* 1998)

5 **Hattersley, Roy,** *The Edwardians* (London: Little, Brown, 2004) 27

Where was God?

'Why, O LORD, do you stand far off? Why do you hide yourself in times of trouble?' (Psalm 10:1)

Rescued crew members from RMS *Titanic* being given dry clothes in New York City, April 1912

'Where was God?' is often the question asked when times of personal or collective suffering occur. But, I wonder how many of those who ask the question even think of, or acknowledge, God's existence prior to the calamity.

Who is to blame?

So often the people who are quick to jump on the 'blame' bandwagon have forgotten all the good things that they have been blessed with prior to the mishap. Indeed, when a tragedy is averted or is a 'close run thing', how often do we see the headline or hear the words: 'God saves!' Instead we so often read or hear of 'a lucky escape' or possibly 'a miraculous escape', with no credit given to the Almighty.

The answer to the question: 'Where was God?' is, of course, that God is with his people, no matter where they are or in what circumstance they find themselves. On the night of 15 April 1912 both those who believed in God and those who did not faced the same fate. The difference was that those who knew Jesus as their Lord and Saviour could know with certainty that they would be welcomed into heaven if they died.

A personal testimony

Several hundred passengers were saved by the operation of a new miracle—wireless telegraphy. In a far greater way, countless numbers have been saved because of a greater miracle. The Lord Jesus Christ gave himself in the place of sinners on the cross. However, it is one thing to know the truth and what action should be taken, but it is quite another to do something about it. Let's imagine one of the victims of that fateful night, while desperately trying to keep afloat in the Atlantic Ocean, seeing, upon looking up, a lifeboat close by which was half empty. Would he or she have reasoned like this: 'There is room in that boat for me, but I wonder whether they will consider stopping to pick me up?' Or, 'I wonder if they are of the same social status as I am? After all, I have to take my reputation into account.' In a moment of such danger, such thinking would be absurd! The person is far more likely to call out, 'Help! Help! Rescue me!'

It is one thing to know that people can be saved by Jesus Christ. It is quite another to call out to him, 'Help! I'm here! Rescue me!' People from all walks of life, from all backgrounds, from all ranks can come to Jesus Christ. He knows no distinctions.

John Harper certainly knew this. So when he fell into the freezing water, instead of blaming God, he swam around trying to help others to be prepared to meet their Maker. When Jesus died on the cross, two thieves were crucified too, one on either side of him. They both faced the same death. They were both given the same opportunity to repent and receive Jesus as their Saviour. Only one accepted him as Saviour and Lord. The other died lonely, forgotten and unforgiven.

As for the few who did make it into the lifeboats, one wonders how many of them praised the Creator for their rescue. Who knows how many of them had heard the Word of God, the Bible, at some time in their life, as going to church was an 'acceptable thing' in Britain at that time? How many, though, had accepted him as their personal Lord and Saviour?

What about those who have never heard of Jesus?

Those who have had the opportunity to hear the good news about Jesus, have the responsibility to respond to him in repentance and faith. But what about all those who have never heard of him and his saving work on the cross? The apostle Paul tells us in Romans 1:20: 'For since the creation of the world God's invisible qualities—his eternal power and divine nature—have been clearly seen, being understood from what has been made, so that men are without excuse.'

The responsibility to make the Lord Jesus known lies with Christians, for Paul also says, 'How can they believe in the one of whom they have not heard?' (Romans 10:14). God was not to 'blame' for the accident. It was not his hand on the ship's wheel that night, nor was it he who sailed the ship full speed into an ice field. No, it was man! Many steps could, and should, have been taken to avert the terrible situation but none were implemented.

In which direction are we heading?

The Bible is the great guidebook for life in the world today; it is a light shining in a dark place (2 Peter 1:19).

In the Bible the greatest warning has been sounded. But have we heard it?

'First of all, you must understand that in the last days scoffers will come, scoffing and following their own evil desires. They will say, "Where is this 'coming' he promised?

Ever since our fathers died, everything goes on as it has since the beginning of creation." But they deliberately forget that long ago by God's word the heavens existed and the earth was formed out of water and by water. By these waters also the world of that time was deluged and destroyed. By the same word the present heavens and earth are reserved for fire, being kept for the day of judgment and destruction of ungodly men.

'But do not forget this one thing, dear friends: With the Lord a day is like a thousand years, and a thousand years are like a day. The Lord is not slow in keeping his promise, as some understand slowness. He is patient with you, not wanting anyone to perish, but everyone to come to repentance.

'But the day of the Lord will come like a thief. The heavens will disappear with a roar; the elements will be destroyed by fire, and the earth and everything in it will be laid bare.

'Since everything will be destroyed in this way, what kind of people ought you to be? You ought to live holy and godly lives as you look forward to the day of God and speed its coming. That day will bring about the destruction of the heavens by fire, and the elements will melt in the heat. But in keeping with his promise we are looking forward to a new heaven and a new earth, the home of righteousness' (2 Peter 3: 3–13).

The Bible also clearly explains that one day everyone who has ever lived will stand before God. We do not know when that day will be, but the question is 'Are we ready?'

Surely we are safe?

One of the saddest episodes connected with the tragedy concerns the lifeboats that were discarded. After all of the lifeboats were emptied, they were hoisted aboard the *Carpathia,* with the exception of the two new Englehardt rafts which were cast adrift at sea. Four weeks after the *Titanic* had sunk, the *Oceanic* was sailing over nearly the same course taken by the *Titanic,* when it sighted an object. A boat was lowered and one of the Englehardt boats was identified. In it were three bodies, one passenger and two firemen. It seems they had been in the water and had seen a raft and managed to get into it. We can only imagine the relief these three must have felt when they thought that they had a chance to survive. Their hope must have turned to despair when no one came to their rescue. Finally, they were probably overcome by fatigue, cold and starvation. They must have thought that they were going to be saved but their hope proved to be false hope. Where is our hope? In what do we trust? Are we certain that we do not have a false hope?

A sad fact but a wonderful hope

All who have lived for a reasonable length of time have at some time faced tragedy: suffering or trials of some sort. Does it hurt? Of course, it does! But, and here is the big *but*, those who know and trust the Lord Jesus as Saviour will know and can experience 'the peace of God, which transcends all understanding' (Philippians 4:7). Even when our world is collapsing all around us, we know that God is with us. This does not make us superhuman. We hurt, we cry, we get scared like everyone else. But we trust and hope in a mighty God, and we are confident that, should we even die, he will pass through the 'valley of death' with us and receive us into his presence.

In the New Testament section of the Bible, the apostle Paul tells us of the great hardship and pain that he endured. He was shipwrecked three times! In spite of all this, he was able to write with confidence: 'For I am convinced that neither death nor life, neither angels nor demons, neither the present nor the future, nor any powers, neither height nor depth, nor anything else in all creation, will be able to separate us from the love of God that is in Christ Jesus our Lord' (Romans 8:38–39).

All Christians have a duty to tell others about the Lord Jesus and his saving work upon the cross until our voices are silenced in this world like the voices of those who perished that night.

A great prayer

'Almighty God, Father of all mercies we, Thine unworthy servants, do give Thee most humble and hearty thanks for all Thy goodness and loving kindness to us and to all men, particularly to those who desire now to offer up their praises and thanksgivings for Thy late services vouchsafed unto them. We bless Thee for our creation, preservation and all the blessings of this life but, above all, for Thine inestimable love in the redemption of the world by our Lord Jesus Christ, for the means of grace and for the hope of glory. And we beseech Thee, give us that due sense of all Thy mercies that our hearts may be unfeignedly thankful and that we shew forth Thy praise not only with our lips but in our lives, by giving up ourselves to Thy service and by walking before Thee in holiness and righteousness all our days, through Jesus Christ our Lord, to whom, with Thee and the Holy Spirit, be all honour and glory, world without end. Amen.'[1]

Prayer of General Thanksgiving, used at the end of the film *A Night to Remember* (1958, Rank Corporation)

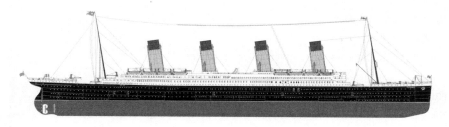

An artist's impression of the *Titanic*

Note

1 Prayer of General Thanksgiving, taken from *The Book of Common Prayer* (1662).

Chronology of events associated with the sinking of the *Titanic*

WEDNESDAY, 10 APRIL 1912

12:00 Noon

The *Titanic* leaves Southampton, England on her maiden voyage.

07:00 p.m.

The *Titanic* stops at Cherbourg, France.

09:00 p.m.

The *Titanic* leaves Cherbourg and sets sail for Queenstown (now known as Cobh), Ireland.

THURSDAY, 11 APRIL 1912

12:30 p.m.

The *Titanic* arrives in Queenstown, Ireland.

02:00 p.m.

The *Titanic* leaves Queenstown and sets sail for New York.

FRIDAY, 12 APRIL TO SATURDAY, 13 APRIL 1912

The weather is good and the sea is calm, but temperatures are dropping. The *Titanic* receives several wireless messages from other ships reporting the presence of ice.

SUNDAY, 14 APRIL 1912

09:00 a.m.

The *Caronia* reports seeing ice at Latitude: 42° N and Longitude: 50° W.

01:42 p.m.

The *Baltic* sends a report warning of ice.

Chronology of events associated with the sinking of the *Titanic*

01:45 p.m.

The *Amerika* reports seeing two large icebergs at Latitude: 41° 27' N and Longitude: 50° 08' W. This message was not sent directly to the *Titanic*, but was supposed to be passed on later when the *Titanic* came within range of a transmitter.

07:15 p.m.

The temperature drops to 39° (F). The warning about ice from the *Baltic* is finally posted on the bridge.

07:30 p.m.

The *Californian* reports passing three large icebergs at Latitude: 42° 03' N and Longitude: 49° 09' W.

09:00 p.m.

The temperature drops to 33° (F).

The crow's nest is instructed by Second Officer Lightoller to 'keep a sharp lookout for ice'.

09:20 p.m.

Captain Smith retires to his cabin for the night.

09:40 p.m.

The *Mesaba* reports pack ice, field ice and icebergs in the area where the *Titanic* is sailing. There is no evidence that this message ever reached Captain Smith or the *Titanic's* bridge.

10:00 p.m.

The temperature drops to 32° (F).

The speed at which the *Titanic* is travelling is 21.5 knots.

Frederick Fleet and Reginald Lee take over lookout duty in the crow's nest. Interestingly, they do not have glasses (binoculars).

10:55 p.m.

The *Californian* sends a wireless message directly to the *Titanic* telling her that she, the *Californian*, has been stopped and is surrounded by ice. The temperature of the water in the ocean is about 28° (F).

11:30 p.m.

Lookouts Fleet and Lee notice a low-lying mist ahead, but do not see an iceberg.

11:39 p.m.

Lookout Frederick Fleet picks up the phone that connects directly to the bridge. Sixth Officer Moody answers the call and is told, 'Iceberg right ahead!'

Appendix 1

Quartermaster Robert Hichens is given the urgent command to turn the ship *hard-a-starboard*. The *Titanic* turns to the left.

11:40 p.m.

The *Titanic* is struck by the iceberg and begins to flood.

First Officer William Murdoch closes the watertight doors.

11:45 p.m.

Captain Smith tells Thomas Andrews and the ship's carpenter to 'sound the ship' (inspect the damage).

MONDAY, 15 APRIL 1912

12:00 midnight

Thomas Andrews informs Captain Smith that the first six watertight compartments have been breached and predicts that the *Titanic* will stay afloat for two hours at the most.

12:05 a.m.

Captain Smith gives the order to his crew to prepare the lifeboats and requests that wireless operators, Harold Bride and Jack Phillips, send the 'CQD' distress signal.

12:15 a.m.

The Cape Race wireless station and the ships *Mount Temple* and *La Provence* receive the *Titanic's* first wireless distress signal.

12:25 a.m.

Captain Smith realizes that the ship is lost and gives the order to start filling the lifeboats—'women and children first'.

12:45 a.m.

The first lifeboat (boat 7) is launched and the first distress rocket is fired.

01:15 a.m.

The water is up to the nameplate on the bow.

01:20 a.m.

The last distress rocket is fired.

02:05 a.m.

The bow of the *Titanic* continues to submerge. The water is almost up to the Bridge deck.

02:10 a.m.

Phillips continues to send distress signals. 'We are sinking fast and cannot last much longer.' The stern is noticeably beginning to rise above the ocean.

02:17 a.m.

The last distress signal is sent from the *Titanic* but it is cut short as the ship's bow plunges beneath the water and the stern rises high above the ocean surface.

02:18 a.m.

The lights blink once and then go out. The forward funnel breaks off and hits the water, crushing anyone in its path.

02:19 a.m.

The *Titanic* breaks into two pieces between the third and fourth funnels. As the bow sinks further, the stern momentarily remains on the ocean surface.

02:20 a.m.

Two hours and forty minutes after striking the iceberg, RMS *Titanic* slips into the sea and begins her descent to the ocean floor.

(Note: There may be some variations, but most agree that the *Titanic* collided with the iceberg at approximately 11:40 p.m. and finally sank at approximately 2:20 a.m.)

04:10 a.m.

The *Carpathia* picks up the first of the *Titanic's* lifeboats (boat 2).

08:30 a.m.

The *Carpathia* picks up the last of the *Titanic's* lifeboats (boat 12).

08:50 a.m.

The *Carpathia* begins its journey to New York with the survivors of the *Titanic* on board.

WEDNESDAY, 17 APRIL 1912

The *Titanic* was scheduled to have arrived in New York at White Star Line's Pier 60.

THURSDAY, 18 APRIL 1912

The *Carpathia* docks at Pier 54, North River, New York with the *Titanic's* survivors on board.

Appendix 1

FRIDAY, 19 APRIL 1912

The United States Senate begins an inquiry into the sinking of the *Titanic*. The inquiry ends on 25 May 1912.

THURSDAY, 2 MAY 1912

The British Board of Trade begins a formal investigation into the loss of the *Titanic*. The inquiry ends on 3 July 1912.

SUNDAY, 1 SEPTEMBER 1985

Robert Ballard's team discovers the scattered wreck and debris field of the *Titanic* in the North Atlantic Ocean, 13,000 feet (2.5 miles) below the surface.

MONDAY, 10 AUGUST 1998

A twenty-ton section of the *Titanic's* hull, measuring 26 feet x 30 feet, is raised to the surface by RMS *Titanic* Inc.

Memorials

Memorial to the *Titanic* in Southampton, erected on the site of the Central City Library. This is one of many that are located across the world

AUSTRALIA

New South Wales

Sturt Park Reserve and Titanic Memorial, Corner Sulphide and Wolfram Street, Broken Hill, NSW 2880: There is a stone column dedicated to the *Titanic's* bandsmen.

Victoria

Sturt Street, Ballarat: There is a bandstand and plaque dedicated to the *Titanic's* bandsmen.

Appendix 2

BELGIUM

Liege: Hotel Cardinal, Place Royale 21 Spa, 4900: There is a small plaque (new 2002) dedicated to the memory of Georges Alexandre Krins, violinist and master of the string orchestra on board the *Titanic*.

CANADA

Nova Scotia: Fairview Lawn Cemetery, Windsor Street, Halifax: This is a graveyard where 121 of the victims of the *Titanic* are buried.

FRANCE

Cherbourg: Cité de La Mer, Gare Maritime, Transatlantique, 5900 Cherbourg-Octeville: A plaque is dedicated to all those who lost their lives (new 1996).

UNITED KINGDOM

ENGLAND

County Durham

Darlington, Priestgate/Crown Street: A stone and plaque opposite the offices of *The Northern Echo* are dedicated to William Stead, a journalist and editor.

Essex

Ongar: St Helen's Catholic Church, 87 High Street, CM5 9DX: There is a memorial stained-glass window dedicated to the memory of Father Thomas Byles, who gave up his place in a lifeboat to stay and offer help to those on board.

East Sussex

Eastbourne: Located at the seafront on the bandstand, there is a memorial plaque to John Wesley Woodward, a cellist with the band on the *Titanic*.

Hampshire

Southampton: Andrews (East) Park, off Brunswick Place: There is a bronze and granite memorial dedicated to the electricians and engineers, all of whom perished in the tragedy (restored 2010).

Southampton: At the Post Office on the High Street, there is a memorial plaque dedicated to the postal workers on board. The *Titanic* had its own Post Office.

Southampton: A new memorial plaque (1993), located at the docks, is dedicated to the passengers and crew.

Southampton: In the Old Burial Ground, West End High Street (opposite the war memorial), lies the unassuming grave of Captain Rostron.

Southampton: Holy Rood Church, High Street, Southampton CM5 9DX: A fountain is dedicated to the memory of the firemen, sailors and stewards.

Lancashire

Colne: Colne Cemetery, Keighley Road: There is a marble pillar and bust dedicated to the memory of Wallace Hartley, bandleader. In 2000 a mural commemorating the sinking of the *Titanic* was unveiled on Parliament Street.

City of London

London: near Fleet Street on the Embankment, there is a plaque in memory of William T. Stead, a newspaper journalist and editor.

Merseyside

Liverpool Philharmonic Hall, Hope Street, Liverpool L1 9BP: A plaque is dedicated to the eight musicians on board the *Titanic*.

Royal Liver Building, Pier Head, Water Street, Liverpool: There is a large pillar dedicated to the engineers (The memorial also includes a dedication to the mariners lost in World War I).

Merseyside Maritime Museum

The first-class ticket of Rev. Stuart Holden of St Paul's, Portman Square, London is on display.

Northumberland

The White Swan Hotel, Bondgate Within, Alnwick NE66 1TD: The First Class Lounge from the *Olympic* is converted into the restaurant at the White Swan Hotel.

Appendix 2

Staffordshire

Lichfield: Beacon Park, Swan Road WS13 6QZ: There is a large bronze statue dedicated to Captain Edward John Smith.

Stoke on Trent: The Potteries Shopping Centre ST11 1PS: There is a new mural commemorating the sinking of the *Titanic*.

Hanley: Town Hall, Albion Street ST1 1QQ: A brass tablet dedicated to Captain Smith is located inside the Town Hall. There is also a plaque on the house where Captain Smith was born in 51 Well Street, Hanley ST1 3PS.

Surrey

Godalming: The Phillips Memorial Cloister, located at the western end of The Phillips Memorial Park (near Godalming Library): This is one of the largest memorials to an individual. It is dedicated to the memory of John George Phillips, one of the wireless operators.

Godalming: The Old Cemetery, Nightingale Road, A headstone in the shape of an iceberg is dedicated to the memory of Phillips. His body was never recovered.

Wiltshire

Melksham: St Michael & All Angels Church, Church Walk SN12 6LX: There is a small plaque (only 16" x 10") dedicated to the memory of Fred and Augusta Goodwin and their six children who were travelling in third class, all of whom perished in the tragedy.

SCOTLAND

Dumfries and Galloway

Dalbeattie: The Town Hall, High Street DG5 4AD: There is a wall plaque dedicated to the memory of First Officer Murdoch in the Town Hall.

Dumfriesshire

Dumfries: Dock Park, St Michaels Street: A stone needle and a plaque are dedicated to the memory of John Law Hume, a violinist in the band, and Thomas Mullin, a steward.

Glasgow: Harper Memorial Baptist Church, Craigiehall Street, Glasgow G51 1EU
www.harpermemorial.net

Ireland

Belfast: Belfast City Hall, Donegall Square, Belfast BT1 5GS: There is a statue dedicated to the crew and workforce of Harland & Wolff. 'Titanic Belfast' is a world-class visitor attraction, located at Titanic Quarter, East Belfast, which is due to be opened in 2012. The building is being constructed over the *Titanic's* slipways and will tell the story from the ships birth in Belfast to its fateful maiden voyage and destruction. For details see www.titanicbelfast.com

County Cork

Cobh (formerly Queenstown): Located in the High Street, there is a stone plaque (new 1988) dedicated to all those who lost their lives.

County Down

The Thomas Andrews' Memorial Hall, 4 Ballygown Road, Comber, Newtownards BT23 5PG: There is a building dedicated to the Harland & Wolfe employee who went down with his ship. It is now used as a primary school.

UNITED STATES

Georgia

The Butt Memorial Bridge, 15th Street, Augusta: A bridge spanning the Augusta Canal is dedicated to the memory of Major Archibald William Butt, aide to the then President Taft.

New York

New York City, South Street Seaport Museum, 207 Front Street, 10038: There is a Titanic Memorial Lighthouse, located at the entrance to the South Street Seaport Museum which is dedicated to all who died in the tragedy.

Manhattan: Main Floor of Macy's Department Store: There is a plaque dedicated to the memory of Isidor and Ida Straus.

Appendix 2

The Straus Park (Broadway and West 106th Street) has a beautiful Memorial Fountain dedicated to both Isidor and Ida Straus.

Bronx, Woodlawn Cemetery, Webster Avenue: This is where the gravesite of Isidor Straus, whose body was recovered, is found. There is also an impressive cenotaph dedicated to the memory of both Isidor and Ida.

Washington DC

Rock Creek Park, Glover Road NW, DC 20015: In the Titanic Women's Memorial, there is a statue dedicated to the brave men who gave up their lives so that the women and children might live.

This list is by no means exhaustive.

Aft: behind, near or towards the stern of a vessel

Astern: in or towards the stern

Bow: the forepart of a ship or boat

Bulkhead: any of the partitions separating one part of the interior of a ship, aircraft, etc. from another

Crow's nest: an elevated platform near the top of a ship's mast where a man on lookout is positioned

CS: **C**able **S**hip

Ellis Island: An island in the Upper New York Bay in Jersey City, New Jersey, where all would be immigrants would be inspected

Falls: a lowering or hoisting rope

Forepeak: the narrow part of a ship's hold, close to the bow

Forward: towards or in the front part of a ship

Greaser: a ship's engineer

Helm: steering apparatus

HMHS: **H**is/**H**er **M**ajesty's **H**ospital **S**hip

Keel: the part of a ship extending along the bottom from stem to stern, and supporting the whole frame

Morse: (a method of) signalling by code in which each letter is represented by a combination of dashes and dots or long and short light flashes

Noblesse Oblige: rank imposes obligations

Port: the larboard or left side of a ship

Prow: the front part, or projecting front part, of a ship

RMS: **R**oyal **M**ail **S**hip

SS: **S**team **S**hip

Starboard: the right hand side of a ship

Stern: the hind part of a vessel

Stoker: a person who feeds a furnace with fuel

Quartermaster: a petty officer who attends to the helm, signals, etc.

Select Bibliography

McCluskie, Tom, *Anatomy of the Titanic* (London: PRC Publishing Ltd, 1998)

Lord, Walter, *A Night to Remember* (London: Longmans, Green and Co., 1956)

Andrews, Carol, *Egyptian Mummies* (Cambridge, MA: Harvard University Press, British Museum Publications, 2004)

Ballard, Dr Robert D., and **Archbold, Rick,** *Lost Liners* (Toronto: Madison Press Books, 1987)

Ballard, Dr Robert D., *The Discovery of the Titanic* (Toronto: Madison Press Books, 1987)

Beesley, Lawrence, *The Loss of the Titanic* (London: Philip Allan & Co., 1912)

Lord, Walter, *The Night Lives On* (Middlesex, England: Viking, 1987)

Wade, Wyn Craig, *The Titanic: End of A Dream* (London: George Weidenfeld and Nicolson Ltd, 1986)

Adams, Moody, *The Titanic's Last Hero* (Belfast, Northern Ireland: Ambassador Productions Ltd, 1998)

Davie, Michael, *The Titanic, The Full Story of a Tragedy* (London: The Bodley Head Ltd, 1986)

Gracie, Colonel Archibald, *Titanic:A Survivor's Story* (London: Alan Sutton Publishing Ltd, 1985)

Eaton, John P. and **Haas, Charles A.,** *Titanic Destination Disaster* (Wellingborough, Northamptonshire, England: Patrick Stephens Ltd, 1987)

Eaton, John P. and **Haas, Charles A.,** *Titanic: Triumph and Tragedy* (Wellingborough, Northamptonshire, England: Patrick Stephens Ltd, 1987)

Geller, Judith B., *Titanic: Women and Children First* (Yeovil, Somerset, England: Patrick Stephens Ltd, 1998)

Useful websites

www.encyclopedia-titanica.org

www.titanic-titanic.com

Picture and photograph credits

The pictures and the photographs reproduced in this book come from a number of sources. Most of them are in the public domain. One is the property of the authors. The remaining ones are from Wikimedia Commons. Use of these pictures and photographs does not in any way suggest that their owners endorse the authors or their use of the pictures and photographs.

The authors wish to thank all those who have placed their work on Wikimedia Commons and granted permission for it to be shared.

Public Domain

Picture 2   The *Titanic* being constructed
Picture 3   The *Titanic* unpainted
Picture 4   Knocking off a Harland & Wolff
Picture 5   The size of the *Titanic's* propeller compared to the size of the yard workers
Picture 6   The *Titanic* at Southampton
Picture 7   Captain Edward John Smith
Picture 8   The *Titanic* leaving Southampton
Picture 9   Lawrence Beesley in the Gymnasium
Picture 10   John Harper and his daughter, Nan
Picture 11   The grand, old staircase of RMS *Olympic*, the *Titanic's* sister ship
Picture 12   The iceberg that may have collided with the *Titanic*
Picture 13   View of the stern and tiller of the *Titanic* in dry dock
Picture 14   Another view of the iceberg suspected of having sunk the *Titanic*
Picture 15   A different view of the iceberg suspected of having sunk the *Titanic*
Picture 17   The last lifeboat successfully launched by the *Titanic*
Picture 19   Jack George Phillips
Picture 20   Survivors aboard the *Carpathia*
Picture 21   The *Titanic's* rescued lifeboats
Picture 22   Map showing the location of the *Titanic*
Picture 23   Account written by the Captain of the *Carpathia*
Picture 25   The *Titanic's* reported position

Picture and photograph credits

Picture 26   Front cover of the *New York Herald*

Picture 27   Captain Smith

Picture 28   Portrait of John Calvin

Picture 29   Rescued crew members being given dry clothes in New York City

Property of the authors

Picture 24   No Pope

Wikimedia Commons

Picture 1   Comparison of the *Titanic's* size with other objects by Yzmo (own work) [GFDL] (www.gnu.org/copyleft/fdl.html)

Picture 16   Cross section of the *Titanic* by DFoerster (own work) [CC-BY-3.0]

Picture 18   Ships in proximity of the *Titanic* by AvelKeltia (own work) [CC0]

Picture 30   Artist's impression of the *Titanic* by Boris Lux (Lux's Type Collection, Ocean Liners—Titanic) [GFDL]

Picture 31   Memorial of the *Titanic*: This file is licensed under the Creative Commons. Attribution: Brian Burnell

Acknowledgements

We would like to thank Ian Cooper and Chris Duncan for their very kind commendations. We would also like to thank Walter Whitelaw of the Harper Memorial Church, Glasgow, and Lee W. Merideth of Rocklin Press for their help with the picture of John Harper. Jim Holmes of Day One Publications has been our greatest help. We thank him for his tolerance and patience.

Pictures and photographs

Every effort has been made to verify all image copyright holders. If we have not done so adequately, this will be rectified in any subsequent printing.

About Day One:

Day One's threefold commitment:

- To be faithful to the Bible, God's inerrant, infallible Word;
- To be relevant to our modern generation;
- To be excellent in our publication standards.

I continue to be thankful for the publications of Day One. They are biblical; they have sound theology; and they are relative to the issues at hand. The material is condensed and manageable while, at the same time, being complete—a challenging balance to find. We are happy in our ministry to make use of these excellent publications.

JOHN MACARTHUR, PASTOR-TEACHER, GRACE COMMUNITY CHURCH, CALIFORNIA

It is a great encouragement to see Day One making such excellent progress. Their publications are always biblical, accessible and attractively produced, with no compromise on quality. Long may their progress continue and increase!

JOHN BLANCHARD, AUTHOR, EVANGELIST AND APOLOGIST

Visit our website for more information and to request a free catalogue of our books.

www.dayone.co.uk

S.O.S. Titanic

JILL SILVERTHORNE

160PP PAPERBACK, 978–1–84625–308–9

Chrissie and Luke Barwell are surprised to find themselves invited on a trip to America by an aunt they scarcely know. Their journey promises more than they expect when they secure a passage on the White Star Line's newest ocean-going liner. Chrissie, though, is uncertain from the beginning about what the trip may hold.

Based on events of April 1912, the journey turns out to be much more significant than any of the travellers could imagine. How will they cope with the life and death situations they face?

Jill Silverthorne was born and bred in South Wales and it was there she committed her life to Christ. She graduated from the University of Leicester with a degree in English and went on to teach at a sixth form college, before leading a faculty and then becoming deputy headteacher in a secondary school in the Midlands. Jill has always loved working with young people in her job and in church settings. She enjoys preparing youth-based resources for holiday clubs, camps and church youth groups. She has been published in association with her work and also worked with several Christian organisations, writing resources for ministries to teenagers. Jill has a passion to see high quality Christian literature written for young people in the twenty first century. This is her first contribution towards seeing that aim fulfilled.

'S.O.S. Titanic' is not one of those books that schools compel you to read, but it is compelling reading. Try it, enjoy it and I suspect you'll not forget it. And even if it's the first book you've read for ages, you'll discover that books can be a delight. This one has dramas within a drama—you'll love it!'
—ROGER CARSWELL: EVANGELIST

Charles Simeon
An ordinary pastor of
extraordinary influence

DEREK PRIME

272PP PAPERBACK, 978–1–84625–313–3

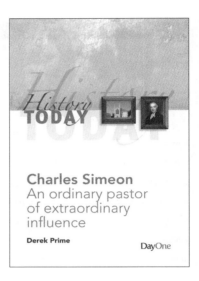

No one had greater influence for the good of evangelicalism in the nineteen century than Charles Simeon and— amazingly—his influence remains, not least in his endurance under opposition and his encouragement and training of young men to teach and preach. Many men— like John Stott— acknowledge their indebtedness to Simeon's example and the pattern he set for expository ministry.

The book aims to be more than a biography. Rather its purpose is to identify and share the teaching Simeon gave concerning preaching and its purpose, and the importance of training young men. It outlines the concern for the Jewish people Christians should have (a subject of contemporary neglect) and the importance of establishing the principle of balance, whether discussing election and human responsibility or any other issue that sadly divides Christians. He explained how often the truth is to be found not in one extreme or the other, or even in the middle, but in both extremes at once.

After serving churches in the UK as a pastor for a total of thirty years—first at Lansdowne Evangelical Free Church, West Norwood, in London and then at Charlotte Chapel in Edinburgh— Derek Prime has devoted himself since 1987 to an itinerant ministry and to writing. He is author of several other books, including *Opening up 1 Corinthians, The Lord's prayer for today, Travel with M'Cheyne* and *Gofors and Grumps,* published by Day One.

Ann Boleyn
One short life that changed
the English-speaking world

COLIN HAMER

144PP PAPERBACK, 978–1–84625–083–5

Anne Boleyn, twenty years old, stepped onto the shore at Dover in the winter of 1521 after several years abroad. She had been sent to France to assimilate French culture, and had used the time well. She was all set to make a big impression at the Tudor court—and did, capturing the heart of Henry VIII.

But this woman, who was in the grave by the age of thirty-six and on the throne of England for only three years, provokes strong reactions from many. Was she an immoral woman who seduced Henry away from his rightful wife for the advancement of family and personal gain? In this well-researched, fresh look at Anne, Colin Hamer sets her in her context as a young woman who had come to true faith in Christ, and shows the impact for good she made from her position of influence, an impact we still benefit from today.

Colin Hamer is currently chairman of a charity that works with the homeless and other vulnerable groups. Following his graduation from Liverpool University in 1972 with BA (Hons), he spent a short time teaching then pursued a business career for more than twenty-five years. He has been an elder at Grace Baptist Church, Astley, Manchester, for twenty years. He and his wife Lois have two adult children. His first book, *Being a Christian Husband—a biblical perspective,* was published by Evangelical Press in 2005.

'Colin Hamer's Anne Boleyn is as exciting as fiction as it carefully makes its way through the historical and religious complexities of Henry VIII's England.'
—DAVID B. CALHOUN, PROFESSOR OF CHURCH HISTORY AT COVENANT THEOLOGICAL SEMINARY, ST LOUIS, MISSOURI

Christmas Evans—No ordinary preacher
The story of the 'John Bunyan' of Wales

TIM SHENTON

176PP PAPERBACK, ISBN 978–1–84625–130–6

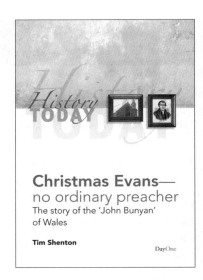

Christmas Evans (1766–1838) was described by D. M. Lloyd-Jones as 'the greatest preacher that the Baptists have ever had in Great Britain'. This remarkable one-eyed Welshman came from humble beginnings to exercise powerful preaching ministries throughout Wales, particularly in Anglesey and the North. In this thoroughly researched biography, Tim Shenton paints an honest picture of Christmas Evans, not excusing or overlooking his faults, but demonstrating how this gentle and humble man, who possessed the spirit of prayer to a remarkable degree, was used by God for the extension of his kingdom in Wales.

Tim Shenton is the head teacher of St Martin's School and an elder at Lansdowne Baptist Church, Bournemouth, England. He is married with two daughters. He has written twenty books, and researched extensively on church history, specializing in the eighteenth and nineteenth centuries. His published works by Day One include *Heroes of revival*, *Our perfect God*, *Jesus in Luke's Gospel* and two other selections of children's daily readings, expositional commentaries on some of the Minor Prophets, *John Rogers—Sealed with blood*, and *Opening up 1 Thessalonians*.

John Rogers—Sealed with blood
The story of the first Protestant
Martyr of Mary Tudor's reign

TIM SHENTON

144PP PAPERBACK, ISBN 978–1–84625–084–2

We in the west sorely need to craft a theology of martyrdom—it would put backbone into our proclamation and living, and help us remember brothers and sisters going through fiery trials even today in other parts of the world. Remembering men like John Rogers is a great help in the development of such a theology. From the foreword by Michael Haykin, Principal and Professor of Church History and Reformed Spirituality, Toronto Baptist Seminary, Toronto, Ontario

teenagers and adults.'
—*JOEL R BEEKE, PURITAN REFORMED THEOLOGICAL SEMINARY, GRAND RAPIDS, MICHIGAN*

'Tim Shenton has produced yet another well-documented, gripping biography of a real hero of faith—John Rogers (d. 1555), renowned biblical editor and first Marian martyr. Follow Rogers's fascinating career from Antwerp to Germany, and back again to England, where he was arrested, remained steadfast under intense interrogation, and paid the ultimate price for confessing Christ. This is a great book about an important epigone; hopefully, Rogers will no longer be marginalized! Highly recommended for

'Shenton weaves a brilliant tapestry from original sources and introduces the reader to many compelling and complex personalities. Well-proportioned in its emphasis, this history will be a vital contribution to studies of Protestant martyrs in Queen Mary's reign.'
—*RANDALL J. PEDERSON, CO-AUTHOR OF 'MEET THE PURITANS'*

James Montgomery
A man for all people

PAUL S TAYLOR

144PP PAPERBACK, ISBN 978–1–84625–209–9

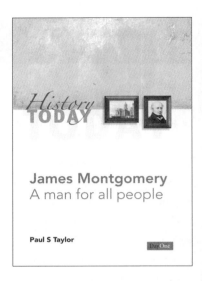

We in the west sorely need to craft a theology of martyrdom—it would put backbone into our proclamation and living, and help us remember brothers and sisters going through fiery trials even today in other parts of the world. Remembering men like John Rogers is a great help in the development of such a theology. From the foreword by Michael Haykin, Principal and Professor of Church History and Reformed Spirituality, Toronto Baptist Seminary, Toronto, Ontario

Paul was for many years an accredited Methodist local preacher and has served the Lord in a preaching and teaching ministry for 55 years. His written works include *Travelling Man* (with Howard Mellor), the life and work of Rev. Arthur Skevington Wood; *Bold as a Lion* (with Dr Peter Gentry), the life of John Cennick an 18th century Moravian evangelist and hymn-writer; *Sleepers Awake—the Gospel and Post Modernism*; and *Charles Wesley – Evangelist.*

The memorial statue to James Montgomery

has been dusted down and re-sited adjacent to Sheffield Cathedral. But who was he, and what were his achievements? Paul Taylor has helpfully provided the answer in this new and long overdue biography. Poet, hymn-writer, journalist, zealous Christian, and agitator for good causes, Montgomery should be better known. Twice committed to prison for comments on sensitive political issues, Taylor has let him loose to edify us.
—*PAUL E G COOK, PASTOR, PREACHER AND WRITER*